A *Letter* to My Daughters

Memories of My Early Years

Edeltraud Seidel Evans

PAGE PUBLISHING
Conneaut Lake, PA

First originally published by Page Publishing 2024

ISBN 979-8-89315-878-6 (pbk)
ISBN 979-8-89315-896-0 (digital)

Printed in the United States of America

For my daughters:

Barbara,
Karen, and
Victoria.

Contents

Figures

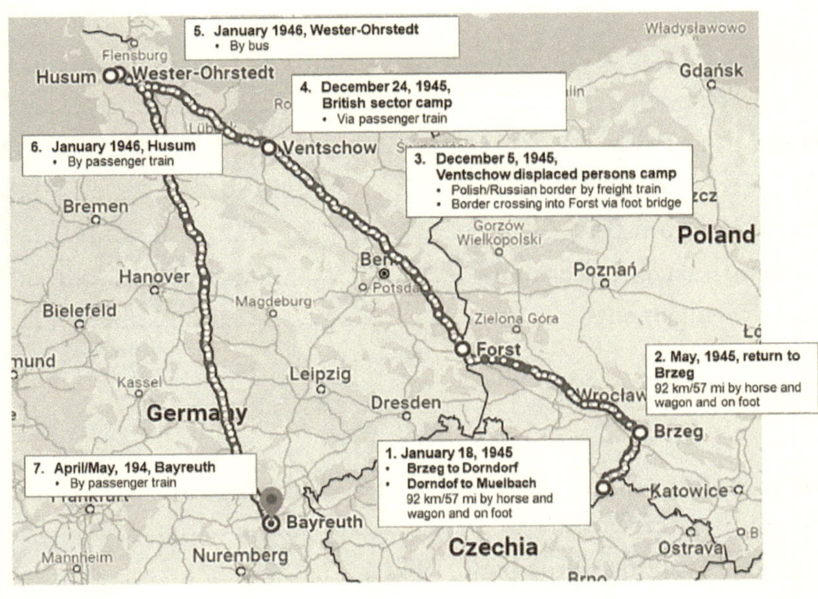

Figure 1: Map showing my family's travels during and after World War II

Preface

One night, I heard a loud knock on the kitchen door. It was very dark in the apartment. There it was again—another knock, accompanied by a loud voice—coming from the front door this time. I was fully awake and alert now. Could it be that Vati had come home, like he had come home once before, in the middle of the night? No, this was not Vati's voice.

Now I could see Mutti in her robe, flashlight in hand, going through our bedroom to see who was knocking at the front door. There was a man speaking harshly to Mutti. "Yes, as soon as possible," I could hear. "There will be trucks taking you to a safe place." Then there was Mutti's low voice, which I could not understand. Then the man said, "No, not for long, only a few days, a week at most." I could hear the door being closed.

This knock on our door happened on January 18, 1945, nine days before Wolfgang's eighth birthday. It would change my life and my family's, as well as many other lives, forever.

Brieg, Schlesien

Our family, the Seidel family—Vati (father), Mutti (mother), Ingeborg (sister), and Wolfgang (brother)—lived at the time of my birth in a small apartment located on Tuchhaus Gasse in Brieg, Schlesien (Silesia), once part of Germany. (Brieg is now part of Poland; the Polish spelling is Brzeg.) The house was adjacent to the Rathaus (city hall). Vati was employed by the city's police department and was eligible for the apartment. I was born there, but I have no recollection of ever having lived there. Mutti told me that I was very sick with the measles when we lived there. I do, however, remember the Rathaus in the center of town called the Ring. It was a beautiful Renaissance building. On the square in front of the building, I remember the statue of King Friedrich der Große II (King Frederick the Great). He had won the battle of Mollwitz, taking back a large section of Schlesien from Österreich (Austria). Wolfgang liked to climb on the pedestal of the statue, but Mutti made him get off right away. My legs were too short, and as much as I struggled, I never could get up.

On the same side of the building were arcades and some shops. One of them sold vegetables and fruit. It was fun running around the column that supported the arcades, playing hide and seek with Wolfgang. There was a large open square on the other side of the Rathaus. We would go sometimes and listen to the military band playing all kinds of music.

When Hitler took over all airports, people who were associated with an airport came under his command. Vati used to enjoy flying gliders. It was an expensive sport, and it caused some friction between my parents, as I later found out. Vati was drafted into the Luftwaffe, the German Air Force. The 1st of September 1939 marked the beginning of World War II. Vati was one of the first men of our extended family to be called up to go. He was one of many invading Poland, known as the Polandfeldzug (Polish campaign or Blitzkrieg). I was three weeks old at the time. I did not know my father until I was about three years old.

Vati loved music and dancing. He taught himself to play the accordion and the harmonica. He had several of them; one was so small it fit into his mouth. The story goes: When Vati was drafted to go to war in 1939, he took his accordion to play to entertain his comrades. They were on a train somewhere in Poland when the train was attacked by Polish soldiers. Shooting everywhere. One bullet went through Vati's accordion. He claimed it saved his life. Mutti always thought it was a great story, but only a story that he made up.

Our new apartment was Mutti's pride and joy. She had found it all on her own. Our new address was Zollstrasse (Toll Road) 30. It was a wide street descending toward the Oder River.

The house was built in the 18th century. It belonged to the Boehm family. The entrance to the house was a big gate-like door. Carriages used to drive through the gate and then to the carriage house in the back. There was also a smaller door we used to enter the house. When we lived there, the carriage house was used as a garage for the owner's car and for storage, like coal bins. The Waschhaus (laundry room) was in this building too. On either side of the front entrance, there was a store. One was an interior design store; the other was a stationary store that belonged to the owner of the house, Herr (Mr.) Boehm. The main house and the carriage house were connected by another narrow house. Servants, like maids, chauffeurs, or gardeners, used to live there. The Tamm family lived in the side house now; Herr Tamm had been drafted. Their two children were older than Wolfgang and me, but Inge made friends with them.

Our apartment was on the Bel-Etage (main floor) of the house. A wide staircase led up to the landing and continued up to the second floor. The owner's brother, a dentist, had his practice and apartment on this floor. Herr Boehm and his wife lived on the third floor. Then there was the attic, which was used for storage and drying laundry.

The original apartment had seven rooms, a kitchen, a bathroom, and a separate toilet. Because of the housing shortage, the apartment was subdivided so three different families could live there. The original renter, an elderly woman, lived in two rooms: the kitchen and bathroom. Herr and Frau Didkofsky had one room with kitchen and bathroom privileges. We always admired the beautiful yellow, green, and brown glass panels on the entrance door to the main apartment.

The Seidel family occupied the other four rooms. Before we moved into the apartment, one of the rooms was remodeled into a kitchen. As German apartments were at the time, all rooms were interconnected. Our apartment had two entrance doors. There was one big, wide double door to the left of the landing, with a bell to one side. This door opened to the living room. Visitors, except Oma (grandmother) and Opa (grandfather), would use this door. The other door was to the right of the landing; it opened into the kitchen. Off to the side, on the landing, were the toilet and a storage room. Mutti kept our bathtub and other items in there.

I don't remember moving into the apartment. I do remember staying with Mutti's friend, Margot. I called her Tante Maugel (Aunt Maugel). I was barely two years old and couldn't speak very clearly yet. Tante Margot's husband had a finger missing from an accident and was not drafted into the army at the start of the war. He liked to tinker and repair things. He overhauled an old sewing machine for Mutti.

He had a worktable in the entrance hall of their apartment. It had two legs and was held up to the wall with hinges. All his tools were hung up on the wall behind the table. When he worked, he would lower the table. He could reach for his tools easily when needed, but they were out of the way when not in use.

Mutti loved the new apartment and enjoyed making it look very pretty.

The kitchen was roomy, with a window and a door leading to the Altane (balcony) outside the back wall of the kitchen. To the right of the kitchen door was the water faucet above a round, bellied cast iron sink. Next to the sink was the kitchen cabinet; it was white and had many drawers, doors, and a breadbox. Then there was the Kachelofen (tiled closed fireplace) we used during the cold season. It had a cooking surface and a water basin, and we had warm water whenever the stove was in use. It also had a bake oven, but it had to be heated separately from the cooking section. Mutti also had a portable, four-burner gas cooker. She set it on top of the stove and used it during the warm season. There was a small space between the cabinet and the Kacheloven. I would sit there on the Ritsche (little footstool) and be warm on cold days.

On one side of the stove on the wall, Mutti kept the Kaffeemühle (manually operated coffee grinder) and the saltbox. Next on this side of the kitchen was a door. It used to lead to the main kitchen of the apartment. Since the apartment was subdivided, the door was made into a pantry. Mutti stored all kinds of pots, pans, and foodstuffs there. She covered the pantry with a pretty curtain that matched the window curtain. This was my favorite place to hide when Wolfgang and I would play hide and seek. Of course, my feet would stick out and give me away.

Along the other wall were the kitchen table and chairs. We would always eat our meals at this table. There was nothing special to see looking at the table, but it was unique. It could be used as a dishwashing station. The two sets of front legs and the connecting piece could be pulled out like a drawer, and like magic, a second table with two enameled dishpans would appear. Mutti would do the dishes in the two bowls, and when done, she would push the table back together again.

Next was the door leading to our parents' bedroom. Beside this door, Mutti kept the Ritsche. She would use it to reach the top of the cabinet, where she kept some houseplants. I also liked the Ritsche. I remember sitting there coughing when I was sick with the whooping cough.

Down the middle, along the length of the kitchen floor, was a linoleum runner. It was dark green in color with a flower design of different colors. Another item Mutti was proud of. Wolfgang and I would move the kitchen chairs on to the runner and pretend this was a train on the track going to the big city or the mountains. We would use the Ritsche and the sewing machine cover as our suitcases. What fun.

Our parents' bedroom was very big. It had two windows opening to the balcony. Between the windows, Mutti had her Frisierkomode (vanity). Then there was the big bed. Two single beds were set together, as it was done in those days. On either side of the bed was a nightstand with pretty lamps. On the opposite side was the Kleiderschrank (wardrobe), where Mutti kept her clothes. In one corner of the room was a chaise lounge. I was allowed to take my afternoon nap there, like a big girl.

Our room, the Kinderzimmer (children's room), connected the bedroom with the living room; it was a long room. Walking into the room, along the left side were our beds. Mine, a crib, was the first closest to the door. Then came Inge's bed; it was a regular twin bed. Wolfgang's bed was bigger than mine, like a youth bed. Across from the beds was a wardrobe and a table with chairs. A piece of furniture I remember most was a cabinet, much like a roll-top desk. It was tall and made of wicker. The top third could be opened by turning a knob. The door would come down and stay in place like a desk, hinged with chains to the cabinet. Inge used to do her homework or her assignments for the Hitler Youth at her desk.

The section below the desk was opened with a double door. This was Wolfgang's space. He stored his toys there. I was not allowed to play with his toys unless he said so.

My portion of the cabinet was a drawer. I hated it. It was so shallow that not much could fit into it. But being the shortest, it only made sense that I should have it. In time, I learned that if I slammed the drawer shut, I would knock over Wolfgang's soldier parade in the cabinet above. It always made him angry, and it was sweet revenge for me!

Most of the time, Wolfgang and I got along very well. I missed him so much once he started going to school.

A double door with glass panels led from the children's room to the living room. There were two large, ceiling-to-floor windows on the opposite wall. Mutti kept several houseplants on the windowsills.

Between the windows was the Kredenz (credenza, or china cabinet), a cabinet where Mutti kept good crystal and other cherished pieces. On one of the long sides of the room was the couch. Next to it, in the Clubecke (conversation corner), there were two upholstered chairs and a corner table with a lamp. The fabric of the chairs was rustic brown with a very pretty flowery print; everyone who came to visit admired them. On the wall to the left of the door, we had a small table with all sorts of family photos displayed.

Then there was the front door. In the corner was a tall Kamin, another closed-in fireplace reaching to the ceiling. The tiles were light beige and sage green in color. In winter, we set our house shoes on the mantle to keep them warm until we came home from playing in the snow.

Next came the door that led to the neighbor's rooms. Mutti had moved a big wardrobe in front of the door, so it could not be seen. In the other corner, by the window, Mutti kept her sewing machine. In the middle of the room were the big table and chairs. That was used when we had company.

This apartment was my world. I have many memories of living there. Some are sad, some are happy, and some are funny.

I always liked to climb on the windowsill in the living room to look at what was going on down below on the street. I was told many times not to since it was dangerous and I could fall out and get hurt, but I could not resist. So one day in May, Oma brought some dead maybugs and scattered them on the windowsills. I did not like maybugs at all, so I was cured!

Vati had sent a stuffed, miniature pony for us to play with. It was attached to a board with wheels. It was fun being pulled around, and sometimes we played too wild and fell off the pony.

One day we got a small package from Vati; there was a letter for Mutti and a large bar of chocolate to share. Mutti broke off two pieces—one for her and one for me. The rest she put on the table in the children's room to share later. Mutti got busy, then wondered what I was doing being so quiet. She found me sitting in the middle of the table, munching on the chocolate. My face was all messy, and only a few pieces were left; I had eaten all the rest! I was not punished, as Mutti realized that this was the first time I had consciously eaten chocolate. I was told never to do something like this again.

Oma (Mutti's mother) lived on the other side of the Oder River in a rural area. We would visit her often. I had very light blond hair, and Mutti always had me wear a hair band. I had many of them, some plain, some with little flowers. One day, while I was still in the stroller, we visited Oma. After we crossed the bridge, Mutti stopped to chat with a lady she knew. Suddenly, she was startled by my loud scream. There was a goat nibbling on the flowers of my hair band! Wolfgang could not keep from laughing; it was so funny to him!

In the summertime, Mutti would take us to Strandbad (a man-made beach with a pool). The city had purchased the property and developed it into a swimming pool for the citizens to use. There was a swimming school, changing cabins, and a lifeguard. When Inge was about ten years old, Mutti enrolled her at the school to learn to swim. Mutti didn't know how to swim, but she wanted us to learn.

At the pool, there was a long boardwalk with poles anchored to it. To each pole was a hook with a cable connected. Attached to the cable was a harness like a life vest. Each boy or girl was fitted into the harness to practice the mechanics of swimming. After several sessions, the lifeguard would lengthen the cable so the student could swim farther out. By the end of the summer, most children were not afraid of the water and could swim. Inge became a very good swimmer; she really enjoyed being in the water.

While Inge was having her lesson, we smaller children would play in the shallow part of the pool. Mutti would always bring surprise snacks and drinks to the pool. Some days we would meet Tante (aunt) Emmy and her four children at the pool. Sometimes one of her friends and children would join us.

We usually walk to the pool, but being the youngest, I got to ride in the stroller. Only after my fourth birthday did I have to walk too. We were always very tired after being in the sun and playing in the water. So Mutti would lower the backrest of the stroller; she had Wolfgang sitting in the back and me in front of him. He was happy not to have to walk the long way home.

One day, as we were walking home, a thunderstorm broke loose. It rained very hard, and we were a little scared. On our way home, we had to walk through a railroad tunnel. We hurried to the tunnel for shelter from the storm. There was so much rainwater that we had to take off our shoes so as not to ruin them.

I loved to play in the water but did not like to get splashed in the face. I would always cry and complain to Mutti about it. One day she said, "It's only water! Don't be such a crybaby." According to the story, I walked off far away from everyone. When it was time to go home, I was nowhere to be seen. "Wo ist unsere Traudel? (Where is our Traudel?)" Traudel is what my family called me when I was a little girl. No one had seen me for a while. They looked everywhere, and everyone was getting worried. Then Mutti spotted me, walking along the edge of the pool. She took off running to catch up with me. She did not call my name, being afraid she might startle me and I would fall into the deep water because I was so close to the edge. I had been crying and had a dirty, runny nose, but I had a few Gänseblumchen (daisies) in my hand. Everyone was happy to see me and was glad I was not hurt. I have no memory of this happening, but it is true. The story was told many times.

I vaguely remember being sick with Ziegenpeter (the Mumps). I had to wear a scarf and stay in bed because of the fever. Wolfgang was sick with it at the same time. Another time I had whooping cough. This I remember because it always made me sick to my stomach when I had a coughing spell.

Tante Emmy, Mutti's sister, and her family had a garden plot. Uncle Günther liked to raise a nice garden. After he was drafted, the garden was worked on by the family. Emmy and Günther's son Herbert, who was two years older than Inge, had learned to work the garden from his father. It was always fun to go to the garden. There were tomatoes, cucumbers, gooseberries, and all kinds of vegetables. We would help water the garden and play with Jochen, Herman, and Helga, our cousins.

Water stations for the garden were centrally located. Everyone who had a plot could get water. To fill the watering can, one would dip it into a concrete barrel and take the water to the garden. We children had smaller cans and would help. There was a faucet attached to the barrel, and it was always filled with water.

Wolfgang had little boats carved out of bark; he liked to float them in the water. One time, one of the boats got away, and as he reached for it, he lost his balance and fell in. We screamed for help. A man from a nearby garden plot came and pulled him out. He was wet and scared, but not hurt.

Our hometown, Brieg, had several parks, a castle, several churches, military barracks, and a Lazarett (military hospital). Brieg was not considered important to the war, so we were never bombed.

Mutti would take us to the Bergel Promenade, a small park in town, for walks.

Figure 2: Walking in the park, 1942

There was a fountain called Das Trickened Mädchen (the drinking girl). It was a tall statue. The girl was holding a cup as if to take a drink.

Other times, we would go to the Stadtpark (City Park). It was farther away, and we would go there Sunday afternoon. We would go spatzieren (strolling or slow meandering). We looked at flowers, fed the ducks in the pond, and had a good time at the playground. When it was still open, we stopped at the garden café for refreshments. There was limonade (bubbly lemonade), ice cream, and cake when it was still available. Sometimes other family members would meet us at the park. There was, of course, Tante Emmy, her children, Tante Gertrud, Mutti's sister-in-law, and her daughter, our cousin Ursula. Our Oma came with us many times.

I loved Oma. She had so many stories to tell! Like the one about how I got my name. When Oma and Opa (grandfather) were young, they owned a farm that once belonged to Oma's parents, our great-grandparents. When Mutti was born, Opa was supposed to record her birth with the local church as Edeltraud Reiter. He, however, could not remember the name and registered her as Frieda Emma. There were several children to be baptized on the same day at the church. When the pastor called her Frieda Emma Reiter, Oma looked around to see who the other Reiter people were. Opa nudged her to get up and take the child to the baptism.

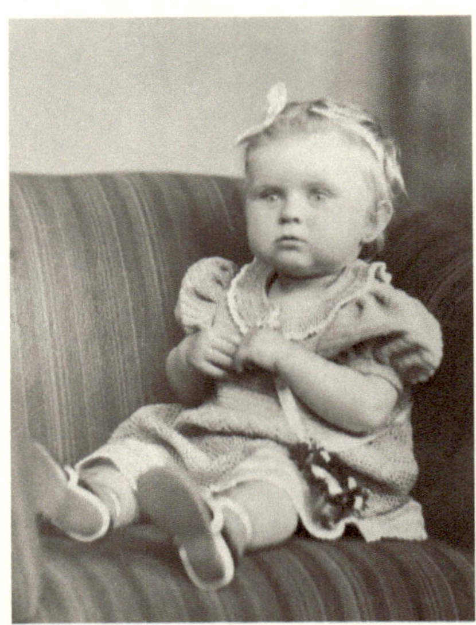

Figure 3: Traditional birthday picture, 1940

Oma loved Opa dearly, and she forgave him for giving the wrong name, so when I was born, Oma insisted that I have the name she liked so much.

Mutti did not remember her father. He was killed in France, on the western front, shortly after the start of WWI in 1914. She was only two years old.

As WWII went on, most of the able men were drafted. Women had to do factory work. Oma had to work in an ammunition factory. She was in her fifties.

Although Brieg was never under direct bomb attack, we had plenty of Fliegeralarmen (air raid warnings). When that happened, everyone had to get off the street and seek shelter. Our house had a large shelter in the lower basement with several bunk beds, a table, and chairs. It was always an adventure for me when we had to go to the shelter.

Inge was caught once on her way home during an alarm. She was taken in by some people until the all-clear was announced. Mutti was very worried about Inge. There was no way of letting us know that she was safe. Very few people had phones at that time; most were taken away by the government anyway.

We often had potato soup with Wienerle (sausage similar to hot dogs) for lunch on Saturday. One Saturday, there were three different Fliegeralarmen. Every time our landlord, the warden, would make sure all the tenants would go to the shelter, on the third alarm, Mutti told Herr Boehm, "We are going to eat and then come to the shelter. This soup had to be warmed over two times; I am not going to warm it up a third time!"

Once we came home from the pool, we had to take cover in the tunnel because of air raid warnings. That was exciting, but not so for Mutti. She was always worried about what could happen. We could hear the airplanes above us, but they went on and probably dropped the bombs on some other city.

I can recall seeing Vati only two times during the war years. He once came home on Kurzurlaub (short leave). Vati was stationed for a long time in Crimea. The Air Force had a R&R facility on the peninsula. Vati had a lot of knowledge about gliders. He also knew how to fly some small planes, like the Fieseler Storch. This got him a position to teach. He taught mostly young lieutenants about gliders and how to fly them. He had the rank of sergeant; it made him feel good to teach the young officers. Vati was lucky; he saw very little actual fighting during the war, only during the Polandfeldzug.

To get home, he had to come back to the Reich—that was what Germany was called at the time by most people, especially by soldiers. Being a resourceful man, Vati found a way to get back to Germany in fewer days than his travel time allowance. He was able to spend several days with us. It was July 1943.

He came home in the middle of the night. When our children got up the next morning, we saw a man lying in Mutti's bed. Surprise, surprise, it was Vati. He had come through Hungary, and somehow he got some goodies, like a very large salami, some sunflower oil, and chocolate. He had also brought some stale Komisbrot bread, specially baked for soldiers.

We had relatives living in Breslau, the big city and capital of Schlesien. We would take the train several times a year to visit them. The train ride lasted for about an hour. It was always exciting for Wolfgang and me. Vati had planned an outing to the zoo in Breslau. He had brought along the stale bread. First, we stopped at Tante Paula and Onkel (uncle) Paul, Oma's relatives' apartment. After lunch, we all walked to the streetcar stop for a ride to the zoo. Uncle Paul was carrying the bag with the bread. He had set the bag down while we were waiting for the streetcar to arrive and forgot to pick it up as we boarded. So at the next stop, he got off, ran back to collect the bag (which was still there), got on the next streetcar, and caught up with us at the zoo. So much excitement!

At the zoo, we finally learned what the bread was for. We were allowed to feed some of the animals. I remember pushing a chunk of bread through the fence, right into a Nilpferd's (hippopotamus) big mouth. When we were tired of walking and looking at all the animals, we stopped at the garden café. Not much food was available because everything by that time was rationed, but we got some cake and lemonade, the fizzy kind. The adults had some Ersatzkaffee (imitation coffee) made from roasted barley with chicory. Wolfgang had some money to spend, and he bought a game called Eselrennen, the donkey race game. Inge and I bought something too; I cannot remember what it was. Wolfgang's game was easy and fun to play. I was very tired by the time we were back home from the big day's outing. Soon Vati had to leave again, but before he did, we had a family photo taken. It is one of the few pictures my relatives had to give us after the war. I look at this picture occasionally.

Figure 4: Family photo, 1943

We had a big teddy bear—so big he could wear Wolfgang's pajamas. One of Vati's cousins and her little son, Dieter, would stop by for a visit at times. We set the teddy on the couch in the living room and told Dieter we would show him something. We made him look through the glass door, and when he saw the big bear, he let out a bloodcurdling scream, being so afraid of the bear. Wolfgang and I got serious talking from Mutti. We could not resist and scared him again at his next visit.

All food was rationed, from bread to potatoes; so were coal, gasoline, cigarettes, fabric, yarn, and shoes—everything. Opa, Vati's father, worked at the Gasanstalt (gas company). He would come visit once a week and bring one or two buckets of coke. Coke is a byproduct of burning coal, and it is used to make gas for heating and cooking, among other uses. Mutti never smoked but would always buy her rations of cigarettes. She would save them for Vati and give some to Opa for bringing the coke.

Vati's mother died in 1935 of cancer. Wolfgang and I never met her; only Inge did.

I had a doll, a Käthe Kruse Puppe (doll). She had molded hair, and I named her Baerbel. She had all kinds of clothes; some Mutti had made for her, others Oma had knitted. On my fourth birthday, I got a really big surprise. Tante Paula and Onkel Paul came to visit. Onkel Paul loved to work with wood. He had made a doll stroller for me. It was beautiful. The outside was painted a sage green with red cherries on either side. The inside was bright red, matching the color of the cherries on the outside. It was one of the biggest surprises I had in my whole short life.

Mutti had baked a birthday cake, and when Oma was making Schlagsahne (whipped cream) to serve with the cake, it turned to butter. She had shaken it too long and too hard; it had turned to little sweet lumps of butter! Electric mixers did not exist at the time.

One day, a large crate was delivered to the apartment. It had a sweet, apple-like smell to it. When Mutti opened the crate, there were two large bags of walnuts and layers upon layers of apples, separated by wood shavings. Vati knew some people in Stuttgart who had a large garden. These kind people had sent the delicious surprise to us. I tried to crack a walnut open by stomping on it. My house shoes had soft soles, and the nut would just slide out and roll away. I chased that nut all over the kitchen but could never crack it. Oma and Mutti had a good laugh. Then they showed me how to use a nutcracker. What an experience! The apples and nuts were shared with family and friends.

My older sister, Inge, was always busy. I saw very little of her. When I was four years old, she was already eleven—practically an adult in my mind. She went to school and had friends. As with all other kids, she became a member of the youth group (precursor to the Hitler Youth). There, she performed all kinds of tasks. During summer vacation, the youth group would work on farms. They even picked up potato bugs. Inge was a bit squeamish and did not like to pick the bugs.

Shortly after Wolfgang started first grade, Mutti was called to the landlord's phone. The school principal told her Wolfgang had an appendicitis eruption and was in the hospital for an operation. Mutti was worried. We hurried to the Krankenhaus Marienstift (hospital). When we got there, Wolfgang was already recovering. The operation went well. The sister put a sack of sand on his belly to keep the wound from breaking open. It made me sad to see Wolfgang in pain. I was happy to be able to play with him once he came home from the hospital. After a few days, he was able to get out of bed and move around. He recovered and went back to school. I was happy for him, but I missed him very much.

I remember Christmas 1943. Vati came home on another very short leave, just a few days after Christmas. On Sylvester (New Year's Eve), my parents gave a party. They invited relatives and friends. Many of them came and enjoyed the festivities. We children were not allowed to stay up late. But we could watch through the glass door connecting our room with the living room. Everyone wore a party hat. There was dancing, and guests would tell stories and jokes. Vati was good at reciting funny poems. There was laughter and singing. Everyone had a good time. After a while, we had to go to bed and never saw the New Year arrive.

Oma had baked Berliner, a kind of filled doughnut. She filled one with a teaspoon full of pepper. She watched who would bite into it. It was Onkel Paul; she saw him bite into it and make a face, but never said a word. Oma was still laughing when she told us about it the next day.

Once, Inge ran away from home. She did not come home after school. Mutti was beside herself. She went to Inge's friends and some of our relatives to find her. No one knew where she was. Inge had gone to Tante Frieda, Mutti's sister-in-law, who lived somewhat out of town. She brought Inge back home. There was a long discussion between Inge, Mutti, and Tante Frieda. I never learned what it was all about.

After this incident, Inge got sick. She came down with a scarlet fever. Dr. Reche, our family doctor, came. She decided Inge did not have to go to the hospital. Inge was quarantined in the children's room. A warning sign was put on each door of the room. Only Mutti was allowed to go in. She had to keep me and Wolfgang out of the room all the time. We slept with Mutti in the big bed. Mutti had to wash her hands and the door handles with disinfectant every time she came out of the room. It was a long time before we saw Inge again. She had lost weight, looked pale, and had dark rings under her eyes. Slowly, she recovered and could go back to school.

Most mornings we would have hot cereal, milk soup, as I called it, and a Brötchen, a small crusty roll, with butter and jam. I did not like milk soup. I would sit and look at it and let it get cold. In the end, I had to eat it if I wanted the roll. One morning, when Mutti was busy making the beds, I hid my bowl of cereal. In the corner behind the door to the balcony, Mutti kept a large kettle to heat water for handwashing laundry. So I hid the bowl in the kettle, closed the lid, and enjoyed the roll. Several days passed, then Mutti used the kettle to heat water. Oh, oh, what a surprise! There was a bow! The cereal had turned green and smelled bad. Of course, Mutti knew who the culprit was. She did not punish me, but I got a lecture on wasting food. Then she remembered missing a bowl one day while doing dishes.

Once a month, Mutti would reserve the Waschhaus. She would have Frau (Mrs.) Walleck come and help with the heavy work. The day before, Mutti and I would go and fill the several tubs with water and then add some soaking powder. Then we would sort the whites from the colored clothes to soak overnight. Mutti would get up early the next morning and start the fire under the kettle. When Frau Walleck came, both women would get busy doing the laundry. I always liked to go and watch or play in the water. At around 9:30, Frau Walleck would have her morning break and eat the sandwiches along with a big cup of coffee Mutti had prepared for her. Frau Walleck would also have lunch with us. She was a robust woman with a hearty laugh. After the laundry was all finished, it was carried to the attic and hung up to dry. When the laundry was dry, Mutti would iron and fold everything to put back into the drawers of the closets. She would fold sheets and pillowcases very neatly and tie the sets together with a ribbon. I got to help by holding down the knot so she could tie a pretty bow.

We had a small basket for kitchen garbage. When I was a big girl, Mutti would let me take it to the cans to empty it by myself. I would empty the basket, set it on the bottom stair, take off my apron, and run up to the corner where Zollstrasse intersected with the Ring. I would watch the traffic and dream of growing up so I could go places.

Life started changing after my fourth birthday, or maybe I became more aware of it. Mutti went more often to the Lazaret. She would take me along. We helped the nurses roll bandages or fold towels and bed linens. Mutti would donate blood to the soldiers who came half dead from the front lines. One of the hospital officials offered Mutti a job. Mutti used to be a secretary, knew shorthand, and was a fast typist, but Mutti turned her down. The lady even offered to get a nanny for us. But Mutti told her, "The children's father is in Russia, and they need me to be home with them to feel safe."

At night, we could hear people walking along our street coming from the direction of the Oder River. We could only see a long line of dark figures moving. All street lights were turned off, and all windows had to be blacked out. No one knew where the people came from or where they were marched to. Several women on our street, Mutti too, would make tea or Ersatzkaffe and pass it out to the people. They were thankful for just a cup of water. Many of the guards would look the other way. Some would tell the women to go home or else.

Mutti had two brothers. The older one, Ernst, was killed early on during the war, I believe in France. I do not remember him at all. Kurt, the other brother, I remember well. He was married to Tante Gertrud, and they had a daughter named Ursula. We called her Uschi; she was about two years younger than me. They lived in the same house as Oma. One day, Oma came by. She was very sad, and she wore a black armband. She gave Mutti a pink sheet of paper to read. That made Mutti and Oma cry. That was a notification that Kurt had been killed in Russia.

He had been wounded and had come home to recuperate just a few months earlier. He didn't want anyone to see him off at the train station when he had to return to his unit. Mutti went anyway; they were very close. He told Mutti that the war was lost and that he would not be coming back. He was right. As I later learned, Mutti knew how bad the situation in Russia had become.

Herr Didkofsky, our neighbor, had a radio he had made himself. This was highly illegal. He asked Mutti to come over and listen with his wife to an underground radio station, but only at night. Here, they learned the truth about what was going on. They knew that all the talk about victory on all fronts, especially in Russia, was a lie. If caught listening to this station, they would have been severely punished.

As the war continued, more people came, mostly at night, through our town. One time after my fifth birthday, I overheard a conversation about how many people had been brought to the banks of the Oder River and were now resting. Some of the people were sick, old, or just tired. They had collapsed with exhaustion. I could not understand how people could collapse. We had collapsible chairs on our balcony; could people collapse like chairs? Mutti explained to me what it all meant.

The winter of 1944–1945 started early and came on full force. First came the snow, and then it turned bitter cold. Even the Oder started to freeze along the banks. We went sledding, but only for a short while because of the bitter cold.

St. Nikolaus Day (Santa Claus) is celebrated on the sixth of December in Germany. Sometimes a friend or relative dresses up as Santa Claus and visits the little children in the family. We always set our shoes neatly beside the bed, so if Santa Clause came while we were sleeping, he would fill our shoes with treats.

In 1944, we celebrated Weihnachten (Christmas) for the last time in our home in Brieg. It was a sad event. We still had enough food and a warm home, but our family and many of our friends mourned the loss of a father, a brother, a son, or a friend.

The toy stores were empty, and people would get mostly home-made presents. Mutti sewed clothes for my dolls. Oma always had yarn, so she knitted hats, scarves, and mittens for presents. Wolfgang had lots of building blocks. He glued them together to make furniture, some chairs, a table, and some beds for my doll house. The doll house was very small; a crate was divided into two rooms and painted. It was lovely. I also got some play dishes, a tea pot, some cups, and saucers. I filled the pot with tea and set it on the mantle of the Kamin to keep it warm. The next day, the tea was gone. It was a mystery to me where the tea had gone. Mutti explained that the tea had evaporated overnight because the Kamin stayed warm all night. Another lesson learned.

Mutti was always saving up kitchen staples and ration coupons for special days, like birthdays and Christmas. She had baked Lebkuchen, a gingerbread cookie, and other cookies for us while Inge and Wolfgang were in school. She had me help cut out the stars and other shapes. Children's rations around Christmas time usually included oranges, sometimes blood oranges from Spain.

We had a lovely Christmas dinner. There was a roasted goose, once a German Christmas tradition. It came from a farm lady who stayed with us for a few days while her husband was recovering from war wounds. He had been shot while on the Russian front. Mutti would often let family members of soldiers who were in the hospital because of being wounded stay with us. It was always fun to have visitors. Oma came and helped prepare the Weihnachtsgans (the Christmas goose). She made the best potato dumplings.

The weather stayed cold, and the snow covered the ground as if to hide the bad news that was coming our way. The year 1944 slipped into 1945 without happy celebrations.

One night, I heard a loud knock on the kitchen door. It was very dark in the apartment. There it was again—another knock, accompanied by a loud voice—coming from the front door this time. I was fully awake and alert now. Could it be that Vati had come home, like he had come home once before, in the middle of the night? No, this was not Vati's voice.

Now I could see Mutti in her robe, flashlight in hand, going through our bedroom to see who was knocking at the front door. There was a man speaking harshly to Mutti. "Yes, as soon as possible," I could hear. "There will be trucks taking you to a safe place." Then there was Mutti's low voice, which I could not understand. Then the man said, "No, not for long, only a few days, a week at most." I could hear the door being closed.

This knock on our door happened on January 18, 1945, nine days before Wolfgang's 8th birthday. It would change my life and my family's, as well as many other lives, forever.

By the time Mutti came back to our room, we were fully awake. Her usual happy face had changed; it was pale and very serious now. She explained to us that the man we heard speaking was from the government and had ordered us to leave our home as soon as we could get ready because the war was coming closer.

Flight from Brieg

e were supposed to go to a certain street on the outskirts of town. There we would meet up with other families and be taken by trucks to villages away from the eastern front, the fighting line, where we would be safe. As Mutti was speaking, we huddled together and cried. Mutti looked at Inge and asked her to be her helper, to be brave and strong.

So Mutti packed, with Inge's help, two suitcases with some of our clothes. As if she knew we would not be back soon, she packed some summer clothes for us too. She also packed our important papers and her jewelry. We dressed in several layers of clothes and the warmest shoes we had.

Standing by the door, ready to go, we turned and said goodbye to our home, not knowing that we would never live there as a happy family again. We walked down the stairs and loaded the suitcases on our two sleds. We started walking the almost endless walk of our lives.

Many other people were walking in the same direction as we were. It was still dark as we came to the assigned meeting place. There, we met our neighbors, the Tamm family. It was so cold, and it seemed to get colder. People were walking back and forth, slapping their arms, and sticking their hands under their armpits to keep warm. I was so tired of standing in the cold that Mutti had me sit on top of one of our sleds.

We could hear the people talking about how long they had been waiting in the cold. Some of the first ones to arrive had been there since 3:00 a.m. No trucks had come to pick anyone up, and night turned into day. Looking behind us, we could see how long the line of people waiting to be transported to safety had become. The line was mostly women and children but also some men, either too old or too young to be drafted, not at this time anyway. Lined up were many sleds, some carts that could be pushed or pulled, and some wagons pulled by horses.

After some more waiting in the cold, people decided to just start walking so we would not freeze to death right there. Slowly, the long line of cold and hungry humans started to move. Setting one foot in front of the other, I hoped the trucks were only delayed and would be here soon and take us to safety. The trucks never came, and our family and all the other people were left to fend for ourselves in the cold.

In a matter of a few hours, we had become Fluechtlinge (refugees).

Little did we know what it meant to be a refugee. Heads down to avoid as much of the cold wind as possible, we kept on walking. Mutti put the two suitcases on one sled and had me ride on the other one, pulled by Inge. She had two blankets in the suitcase and used them now to keep Wolfgang and Inge warm. I will never forget the blankets. They were sage green and brown plaid with a brown binding. I used to cover up with these blankets while taking a nap in the chase lounge.

Wolfgang was so heavily dressed he could hardly walk, so he gave his blanket to Mutti to keep her warm. After a while, I had to walk again so Wolfgang could ride on the sled for a rest. Some kind people, who had a wagon pulled by a horse, gave some small children a ride while sitting between their own children and belongings. I was one of the lucky ones. I could hardly believe it when the women called out to Mutti, "Die Kleine kann mit uns für eine Weile im Wagen fahren" (The little one can come and ride with us in the wagon for a while)." Wolfgang got a break; he got the sled all for himself for a while. All too soon, I had to give up my spot in the wagon so another little child could ride for a while. Later on, Wolfgang got to ride in the wagon; it was a real treat for him.

This went on all day. I do not remember if or what we had to eat. I do remember it getting dark again and stopping at a village.

When I got off the sled, I could hardly walk, being so stiff from the cold. The village refugee coordinator had assigned places for people to spend the night out of the cold. We were lucky to stay with a kind lady in her warm house. Others had to sleep in barns or basements, happy to be out of the cold. The farm lady gave us hot soup to eat. She showed us a room with a large bed. Big enough so all four of us could sleep in it.

The next morning, we found a man, a stranger, sleeping in the bed with us. He was a soldier and a messenger. He had come to the farm in the middle of the night. He stopped to find a place to rest and get some food. So Mutti, Inge, and the farm woman brought him into the house and put him in bed with Wolfgang and me. We were so sound asleep that we never woke up until the next morning. The soldier was so grateful for the food and restful sleep. Then he was gone again. We never knew his name, where he came from, or where he was going.

The following day, we were on the road again. Snow still covered the roads, and it was frigid and windy. Our coordinator told us we had to move to the next village, where we would be directed to farms where we could get food and housing.

This is how we ended up in a small Dorf (small village). Our family was sent to Bauer (farmer) Grindel. He was a kind man. His wife had passed away, and his son was a soldier. There was also a maid, a young woman named Gretel, who kept the house and did the cooking. Because most of the young men had been drafted, prisoners of war were assigned as Knecht (farm hands) to help with the work. Posa, farmer Grindel's farm hand, came from Ukraine.

Now we have a new home. It was one room, die Auszugstube, a room that was designed for when the farmer and his wife retired to live in. Most farm houses had such a room. The room was warm when we walked in. The room was simply furnished: two beds, some chairs, a table, and a Schrank. Above one of the beds hung a holy picture. We shared the two beds. They were big enough for two people. Cozy feather pillows and covers kept us warm at night. In the corner next to the door was a Kamin, similar to the one we had in our living room at home. There was a bench built into the wall facing the fireplace. Several pillows made it comfortable to sit and be warm. I have only good memories of staying at farmer Grindel's home.

It was decided that we would eat our meals together with Bauer Grindel and his helpers, Gretel and Posa, in the kitchen. There was a hallway from our room to the kitchen, which made it convenient for us to go there and eat. Mutti would go to the kitchen and help prepare breakfast and all the other meals. Gretel was happy to have a woman in the house to talk to. Mutti was worried as we had had no news from Vati for a long time, and she did not know where the rest of our family were. Gretel would console her. Gretel and Mutti got along well.

Here we celebrated Wolfgang's eighth birthday. It was a small celebration—a little cake, but no presents. We were warm and had enough to eat, which was a blessing.

One day Bauer Grindel called me into his Gute Stube (living room) and handed me a teddy bear, saying, "Here," he said, "a little girl should have something to play with." Then he reached behind his back and handed me a small suitcase-like leather bag. "Open it," he said. There were all kinds of clothes for the bear. I was so surprised; I did not know what to say. I ran into the kitchen to show Mutti my treasure. She had me go back to thank Bauer Grindel for the lovely gift. From this day on, the bear was my constant companion. I named him Teddy. I played with him all the time. I changed his outfits, took him for walks, and had him sit with me on the bench at mealtime. He slept with me or sat in front of the fireplace with me.

Later, we learned that the beloved bear belonged to the farmer's daughter, who had died at a young age.

I do not know how Mutti managed to keep us warm and clean. She handwashed all our clothes and hung them by the fireplace to dry. I had a Zipfelmuetze (knitted hat with a long point) that Oma had knitted for me. It was one of the presents I received for Christmas. It was light blue in color with red trim. It kept me cozy and warm.

One cold day in February, Bauer Grindel told us that he had planned on butchering a pig in a few days. Several women and men came to help. We were told to stay away from the barn while they butchered the animal. Wolfgang would have liked to watch, but

Inge, Mutti, and I were happy to wait. After a while, men brought big chunks of meat into the kitchen. The pieces were cut up for smoking and curing. Some of the meat was ground up and made into sausage and bratwurst. It was the meal of the day: sauerkraut, sausage, and big chunks of bread and mustard. We also drank some of the Wurstsuppe, the broth the sausages were boiled in. It all tasted very good. Then Posa asked to cook the liver as they did in his home in Ukraine. After it was cleaned and seasoned, he roasted it in the fire after the flames had died down. Another treat everyone enjoyed.

It seemed we had found a home away from home. We had good food and a warm place to live. Wolfgang and I played together and felt safe. Some days we would climb into the hay loft, or Posa would put us on the back of a cow to ride around in the barn. He gave us fresh milk right out of the cow, warm and sweet.

Inge, who was thirteen years old, and Mutti worried about Vati; we had not had any news from him for months. There were no newspapers available, and no one had a radio to listen to. Anyway, the news was only propaganda to make people feel good.

On the day of our deportation, Oma had stayed with Tante Emmy and her children. They lived in a different part of town. They had to leave too, but go to a different pickup location than ours. This made Mutti worry, not knowing where all our relatives were.

There was Opa, Vati's father; he lived out of town, and we did not know where he was either. Vati had two sisters, Margarete and Charlotte, but we called them Gretel and Lotte. He also had a brother, Willi. He had been drafted into an army "Panzer" (tank) division. Gretel's husband was a musician and played in a military band. He was sent to Spain and was killed. Lotte had been married to a Communist; he was in jail for his beliefs. Lotte had moved to Berlin, where no one knew about her husband.

We were living away from home, but the war was still going on. The future of Germany and the German people was decided by the allies.

February 4–11, 1945
Historic Yalta Conference

Also known as
Crimea Conference
Code Name
Argonaut

The purpose of the conference was the reorganization of Germany.

Attended by:
President Franklin D. Roosevelt, USA,
Premier Minister Winston Churchill, Great Britain
Soviet Premier Joseph Stalin, USSR

So life went on. The adults worried about what would happen next. After a few months of living in farmer Grindel's house, our lives changed again.

Once again, a refugee coordinator came to our door. He apologized for the bad news he had to give us. He had to tell us that the war was coming closer and all the refugees had to go to a safer place. This time, we were transported in a horse-drawn wagon. Our belongings were few. Of course, Teddy was my main concern. I held him close to me during the ride to our destination, Mühlbach (mill creek), a small village close to Seitenberg, a town in the Glatzer Schneegebirge (Glatzer Snow Mountain Range, which is now Králický Sněžník, Czechia).

We had to share our new home with other families since we were housed in the school building. The one-room school was now used as a refugee camp. We had none of the comforts we experienced at Bauer Grindel's house. We were assigned two sets of bunk beds. They were in the corner to the right of the door to the classroom. We had no chairs, no table and no lamp—just four beds and the personal belongings we brought with us. Our suitcases fit under the beds. That was it. The teacher, who used to live upstairs, became a soldier.

There were several locked rooms upstairs, as well as a large kitchen. The mothers were allowed to use the kitchen and worked out a schedule so every family could have some time to cook and eat there. Since all the food was still rationed, cooking became a small chore.

Our beds were set up perpendicularly. This gave us a little more privacy. I got the lower bunk along the blackboard. Lucky me. I could use the ledge where the chalk was kept as a shelf. Of course, Teddy was with me day and night. Slowly, we settled in and made the best of the situation. Occasionally, a bus would go to Seitenberg. Mutti and some of the other mothers would go and see if they could find something useful in the stores. They were happy to bring home some yarn to mend our socks and, of course, food. Whatever was available, that is what we ate.

We did not see much of the Tamm family while living in Doerndorf, but they were our close neighbors again at the camp.

Most of the children were happy not to have to go to school. We played outside when the weather was good. There were some books to read, but no drawing paper, pencils, or crayons. I had to keep an eye on Teddy; several of the little girls would have liked to have him.

One day, when snow was still covering the ground, the Förster (forest ranger) came to the camp. He offered to take some of the children to look for deer in the woods. We could go in a horse-drawn sled. He warned us not to make any noise and frighten the deer. We sat all bundled up and waited for the deer.

Here they came—several mothers with their fawns! The forester had set out a salt lick for deer but had nothing else to feed them. He told us that the deer should have been heavier, but they were under-nourished like humans.

After the cold winter, spring, with warmer days, arrived. We were able to play outside in the sunshine. Since we did not have any toys besides Teddy, we made up games. One we particularly liked was tossing pebbles into the creek. We would watch the little stones make big rings in the water. We had to promise not to go too close to the edge of the creek. The little creek carried a lot of water from the recent snow melt. Sometimes we would see a Forelle (trout) swimming by. We let little pieces of bark float in the stream, pretending they were big boats like we used to see in the Oder River back home.

There were several narrow bridges crossing the stream to the farm houses. As I was walking along the creek by myself, I noticed a white speck under one of the bridges. As I came closer, I could tell it was an egg. Quickly, I picked it up and started to run. Well, the egg belonged to a goose. She saw me take the egg and chased after me, squawking and flapping her wings. She never caught up with me. We enjoyed the egg. Mutti hard-boiled it and sliced it so we could share it. Such a treat!

As temperatures got warmer, we played more and more outside. We would lay on our stomachs close by the little creek, looking into the water and watching for fish. Wolfgang tried to catch them with his hands. He tried and tried, but with no luck. One day a trout came by, and quickly Wolfgang reached for the trout and caught it. He was so proud! Mutti cooked the fish for our next meal. Wolfgang got the biggest piece as a reward for catching the fish. What a treat!

I had collected all kinds of different little treasures. There were shiny pebbles, pine cones, odd-shaped sticks, some pieces of bark, and different leaves. I had them all lined up along the chalkboard. I had Teddy watch over my treasures so no one would disturb my collection.

We still had no news on how the war was going. No one could get mail or newspapers; everything was shut down. All the women could do was worry about their husbands and relatives. Families had been torn apart since people were told to go to different places.

We thought of our relatives a lot and remembered Oma's stories, like the one when she was a very young girl on the farm. She and her friends would go for walks in the evening. As they passed the house of an elderly couple, they decided to sneak into the backyard and pick some ripe pears from one of the trees. When she got home with her treasure, her father got angry at her for stealing and made her take the pears back. The old couple was happy someone wanted the pears and to take them back home. Oma refused; she told the couple, saying, "My father will only make me bring them back to you again."

So the days went by, and women worried and did the best they could to take care of the children. We children played. The had given up asking when we would be back home again. They knew the answer by now; no one knew.

Der Krieg ist zu Ende. The war is over. These are the words that blared out of the loudspeaker on top of an old car. People looked at each other in disbelief, but there was again the voice saying, "Der Krieg ist zu Ende."

Victory day for the western allies. Germany had capitulated on May 7, 1945.

> On May 8, 1945 the unconditional Surrender
> Agreement was signed by the western allies at Rimes, France:
> USA, Great Britain, France, and Australia, also an ally.
> General Jodel signed for Germany.
> On May 9, 1945, a separate surrender agreement was
> Signed with the USSR in Berlin,
> General Keitel signed for Germany

"What next? What should we do?" was the most often heard question in our camp. A decision was made by the USSR: all refugees had to return to their hometown by June 1, 1945. But how were we to get back to Brieg without transportation? Traveling by train or bus was not possible. Some of the women, including Mutti, got to know several villagers. One older couple had an old horse, a wagon, and a farm hand. He was a prisoner of war who liked the couple. The women pooled their money and persuaded the couple to rent the set-up and driver to take us back home. Frau Tamm had relatives in a town on the way to Brieg. This is how far the couple was willing to let the farm hand take us. They didn't want any money, so the women gave it to the farmhand.

Back To Brieg

One more time, we packed up our few belongings for another walk, this time back home to Brieg. I was allowed to bring Teddy, but I had to leave all my other treasures behind. I thought about how nice it would be to be back sleeping in our own home.

I can't remember the name of the town we were going to, but I remember being stopped by Russian soldiers several times. They let us pass after the women explained somehow that we were refugees on the way home as ordered.

We only spent one night at Frau Tamm's relative's house. The owners had fled too and were not back yet. The only thing I remember about the house is that it had a door flush with the ceiling in the upper-floor hallway. The Tamm boy had figured out how to open the door. He pulled down the ladder, and we all climbed up into the attic. We were laughing and having a good time when, soon, a stern voice told us to come down or else. After all, this was not our house.

We had some potatoes and fruit in jars we could eat. After breakfast, the driver left with the horse and wagon. Frau Tamm and Mutti worried about the man, hoping he would make it back home safely.

We started walking on the country road toward Brieg, toward home. We were maybe five or six miles away from the outskirts of Brieg. It was a long way to walk with hardly any food or water. I was so tired that my short legs just did not want to move anymore.

Once we got to Brieg, we were told by the Russian guards to find a place to stay at a Siedlung, a housing development on the edge of town. German people were not allowed back into their homes in town. We were so disappointed not to be able to go and sleep in our own beds. Of course, the adults were worried about many other things.

So we had to walk some more to find a place to stay, at least for the night. There were several homes along the road. We stopped at the first one that was open. Frau Tamm and Mutti found it suitable, and so we stayed. There were many other people walking the road looking for a place to stay. Not long after we had settled in, other people stopped. We shared what little food we had with them. They looked in all the rooms and decided to leave without saying thank you or goodbye. We never knew their names.

Behind the little house was a lawn with a bench, some trees, and flower beds. The grass had not been cut, and it had grown as tall as the bench. We children were allowed to play in the grass until it was time to go to sleep. Europe was on daylight savings time, so the days were long.

All at once, we could hear trucks moving along the road. Columns of Russian trucks stopped along the road. Several soldiers jumped out of each truck. Some brought food into the house. Others came into the house, bringing bottles of vodka, and started to drink. One soldier called the women into the kitchen and said, "Frauen komm! (Women, come!)" as he pointed at the food. Frau Tamm and Mutti got busy cooking. There were also nice soldiers who gave our children food. One of the young soldiers was watching Inge. She was thirteen years old and starting to develop. Mutti kept a close eye on her. Nothing happened to Inge.

It got to be bedtime, and we were so tired that we went to sleep right away. Mutti had Inge sleep in the bed against the wall with me laying in front of her.

When we woke up the next day, our Mutti was gone. Inge tried to comfort us as best she knew how. The house was in a mess. Some of the soldiers were lying on the floor and passed out because of too much vodka. Others slept in the trucks.

Mutti was nowhere to be found. We were scared and did not know what to do. Wolfgang slipped out of the house. He went looking for Mutti. After a while, he came back and nodded to Inge. He whispered something to her, and Inge told me not to cry anymore and that it would be fine real soon.

The order came, and the soldiers had to pack up and move out. It was quiet in the house now. Then the Tamm family left. They had relatives in a small village not far away from Brieg; that's where they planned to go. We never saw them again. We waited awhile and then left.

Wolfgang had found Mutti in an abandoned house. As I got older, I learned Mutti had run into hiding because of a soldier who had ill intentions. He kept Mutti sitting on her knees, trying to make her drink vodka to get her intoxicated so he could take advantage of her, maybe even rape her. She pretended to drink the vodka but poured it in the flowerpot behind the chair he was sitting in. At the right moment, she ran out of the house and hid in the tall grass under the bench behind the house. She could hear the drunk soldier stumbling around and yelling, "Frau! Frau!" Mutti did not move; he never found her. After all was quiet in the house, she carefully left her hiding place and found another house, where she spent the rest of the night. Wolfgang went searching for her and found her in her hiding place. She made Wolfgang promise not to tell anyone, not even Inge or me, where she was. Just to say not to worry, everything will be fine again soon. Wolfgang made us wait until the house was empty of people before he told us where Mutti was. Oh, what a joy when we had our Mutti back again! This is how Mutti saved herself from being raped by a Russian soldier.

We were all together again. We moved to another house away from the main road. We decided to make this two-room apartment our new "Zuhause" (our new home). It had two bedrooms, a nice bathroom, a kitchen, and a small entrance hall. No water, gas, or electricity. There were some pieces of furniture, like beds without mattresses, chairs, a table, a kitchen cabinet, a wardrobe, and a cook stove. As mattresses, we used sacks filled with straw. Best of all, we found a very large chunk of salt—yes, cooking salt—in the middle of the floor in one of the rooms. We had no idea how it got there, but we were happy to have it. As we later learned, salt at this time was as good as gold. There were no stores to go to and buy food or other supplies, so finding anything nonperishable was a good find.

For the next few days, we went looking for food and other stuff we might be able to use. We stayed close in the neighborhood. One house we walked into smelled sweet like apples, but it was empty except for a large trunk, which is where the smell came from. Once we opened the trunk, we saw many apples but many more maggots. We dropped the lid and ran. I cannot remember what we ate on those days. To have water to wash and cook with, we had to carry buckets to the Ruestergraben, a creek that ran along a cemetery. It was such a struggle! Mutti was afraid the water was contaminated. We had to boil all the water to make sure not to get sick. There was also a bucket of water in the bathroom to flush the toilet. We had to carry a lot of water every day.

All the row houses in the development had basements. Each apartment had a section that was fenced off and had a gate. There we found coal, firewood, and some potatoes in a bin. All the doors were unlocked, and the keys were gone.

Just days after we moved into the house, another family moved into one of the ground-floor apartments. Their name was Marschall. There was a boy named Hans, older than Inge, maybe fifteen years old, and another boy, about ten years old, and a little girl. The mother kept her away from everyone, so we hardly ever saw her.

We had another neighbor living in the apartment across from ours on the second floor. Her name was Frau Groher, and her little girl's name was Helga. They had lived there when we moved in, but she was afraid, so she stayed very quiet in her apartment. She was a very kind woman. Mutti and Frau Groher became good friends. She was from a farm and taught us many useful things.

Sometime later, another family moved into the apartment below ours. They never spoke to anyone in the house, so we did not know anything about them.

Most German women were called off the streets by Polish soldiers to work for them, clearing rubble and cleaning houses of trash. So was Mutti.

After a few days, Russian soldiers made the women go with them to Moll, a company known for processing hides into leather. The hides were layered in deep pits along with tanning solutions. Men climbed into the pits, hooked the hides on to cables, and men above pulled the hides out of the pits and hung them on racks. The women had to scrape the hair off the hides. The tanning solution turned the palms of the workers hands dark brown. So when a Polish soldier would call, "Frau komm arbeit! (Woman, come work!)," the women would show them their hands and were let go to go to Moll.

All the workers at Moll got a midday meal and a pound of bread. Many of the women would save some of the food and bread to take home. So did Mutti. It was hard work, but her brown palms protected her from having to work for Polish soldiers. We children were left on our own.

Food was our main worry. We went to the Russian mess hall and begged for food. Most of the cooks were kind to us. I carried a milk jug with a handle. The cooks knew we were hungry and gave us some food. Not wanting to get caught by their superiors, they put a chunk of meat or a hamburger patty in the bottom and covered it up with mashed potatoes or some vegetables. Something the soldiers gave us often was sauerkraut soup. It had a tangy taste, and I loved it. It was cooked with plenty of oil. We would let the soup settle and skim the oil off the top to use for cooking.

Mutti had told Inge to stay in hiding as much as possible because of the young soldiers. She usually did, but she watched when I went asking for food. Some days we would boil potatoes, mash them, form patties, and cook them on the stovetop—no fat, no pan.

Wolfgang and Hans got along well. They managed to build a cart to transport stuff. They had found the bottom part of a stroller with all four wheels. Next, they nailed some boards together like a crate and tied them to the stroller frame. No more carrying water from the creek; we used the cart! The two boys were inseparable. They would scavenge for anything usable, like potatoes or vegetables, flour, sugar, or anything that was not spoiled.

Teddy was still my best buddy. I had to leave him at home when we went out, so no one would take him from me.

All the keys to the apartments and the front and back doors were gone. To make the house safe, especially at night, the boys found a heavy beam. They fitted it against the bottom stair and below the door handle. It was almost impossible to open the door from the outside. We would call or toss a pebble against the window to be let into the house. It was awkward, but we were much safer.

One Sunday, when Mutti did not have to work, she and Inge went to where we used to live on Zollstrasse. They took the wagon in hopes of bringing some of our things from home. We could tell that something bad had happened just by looking at their faces and the empty cart as they returned. The house and several others along the street had been almost destroyed by fire. Just the walls were left. Some of the kitchen sinks could be seen hanging from the walls. The entrance was blocked with trash and rubble. One of the neighbors from down the street happened to come by. She told Mutti how the Russians emptied out all the houses and sent the goods in crates to Russia. That angered the Polish soldiers because not much was left for them to take, so they burned many of the houses down.

Mutti and Inge, with the help of other people, had cleared away the rubble and climbed down into the cellar. They found some coal and briquettes, but not much else. What a disappointment it must have been for Mutti and Inge to see ruins where once our home and life were. It was a very sad day; our home and all our beautiful belongings were gone.

Life went on. Mutti had to go back to Moll the next day, and we children had to do the best we could on our own.

The apartment development was designed in a square. Each building had five front-door entrances and six apartments in each section. In the center of the square, there was a playground. One could see that there were benches and play equipment. All that was left now were the sand box, the trees, and the shrubs.

Our new address is Scherf Strasse 3.

One day, people were running down the street, yelling that a horse had fallen and a soldier had to shoot it. We never ate horse meat before but would have, but we were too late, and it was all gone by the time the boys got there.

Clothing was another problem. We had so little, and it was getting threadbare.

By now, we had running water, even though it was sporadic, and we still had to fill our containers. We still boiled all our drinking water just to be safe. There was very little soap, either to clean ourselves or to wash clothes. We had to wash our things almost daily.

Most days, we went barefoot to save our shoes for winter.

Mutti worried about what we would wear when winter came. We had outgrown our winter clothes. I could fit into Wolfgang's things. Inge and Wolfgang were not so lucky.

The workers at Moll decided to steal some of the leather. Most women carried a handbag. Mutti's bag was made of braided twine, and it had a double bottom. Some of the women made a double bottom for their bags. The workers were not watched all the time. Whenever possible, one of the men would cut pieces of leather to fit between the two bottoms of the bags. Some women would hide pieces of leather in their underwear. One man rolled up a hide and tossed it over the fence, but he was caught. On the way out after work, guards watched the workers leave. They would call one or two workers to check their bags. After this incident, the guards looked a little more closely. It was a formality most of the time. The leather was great for bartering.

An old man, a cobbler, lived across the way. He would put new soles and heels on our shoes for a piece of leather. Women would do sewing, mending, or knitting if they had the materials to work with. They would also take leather as payment. Mutti had a stack of leather hidden away; she used it sparingly.

The new commander for Moll was a young officer. He had brought a young woman to live with him. Her name was Mara, and her homeland was Ukraine. The commander asked Mutti one day to help Mara. They lived in a house on the Moll property. The young women didn't know anything about keeping house. Mutti taught Mara about cleanliness and about some of the tasks that were the norm for housekeeping, like how to use a curtain rod or what a flush toilet was for.

The water tank in the toilet was installed just below the ceiling. It had a lever with a chain attached to it. The tank and the bowl were connected by the water pipe. By pulling the chain, the water came rushing down the pipe and flushed the bowl clean. Young Mara was not familiar with a flush toilet. She tried to use it to wash the potatoes in the bowl. She would pull the chain, and the potatoes would flush. She pointed to the toilet, saying, "Zappzarap," meaning, "This thing is stealing my potatoes!" They had a good laugh after Mutti explained to her about the use of a toilet. We, too, had a good laugh when we heard the story. Mara was very good to Mutti. She gave her extra food and clothes. She was grateful for all the things Mutti taught her.

After several months, all the leather at Moll was processed, and the women were told not to come back the following week. The men had to return to work to dismantle the machinery and pack it all up for shipping to Russia.

The commander had all the workers and their families come for a farewell meal. We enjoyed some good food that day.

> July 17–August 2, 1945
> Potsdam Conference
> Attended by:
> President Harry S. Truman, USA,
> Premier Joseph Stalin, USSR
> Prime Minister Winston Churchill
> Former Prime Minister Clement Attlee, UK

The conference was held to decide how to administer Germany, which had agreed to an unconditional surrender. It was also the goal of the conference to establish post-war order, address peace treaty issues, and counter the effects of war.

Of course, we did not know anything about the conference or the decisions the allies had come to about Germany.

At the time Mutti was working at Moll, one of the housing blocks in our subdivision was allocated for Russian officers to use as billets. Mutti found work there after Moll closed. She got to work in the mess hall kitchen. There was no better place to work; the kitchen meant food. The cooks were generous, and we didn't have to go beg for food again.

We also have electricity now. It came on only in the evening and was turned off again after a few hours. One evening, we heard a loud, rumbling noise. We ran to see what it was all about. A Russian tank rolled down the street with several soldiers sitting on top, singing and drinking. They were happy because they were going home. They passed out thick slices of bread with chunks of butter on top. Not all Russians were mean or cruel.

We felt safer with the officers living close by. I was allowed to go out by myself, but only up the street to see Mutti at work or to the playground, where I could be seen from the kitchen window. Usually, I went to the playground.

One day I walked to visit Mutti at work with Teddy in my arm. Down the street was a pushcart loaded with junk and boards. Curious, I walked a little closer. Two women came out of the house, yelling at me and ripping Teddy out of my arm. As I was running to get Mutti, I saw the woman hiding Teddy in the cart. Some of the officers knew how to speak some German and Polish. Mutti quickly told one of them about what had happened. He came with us and made the women hand over Teddy. He also told them to stay in their part of town and never come here again.

My birthday, on August 9, came and went without a big party. I was six years old now and understood how difficult our lives had become.

Russia decided to open schools for German children. I was so excited to be going to school. First graders would go to one of the empty houses in the neighborhood. We had a nice young woman as a teacher, but not much else. She would teach us the alphabet, how to count, and how to write our names. We learned some songs, and she would read stories out of the few books she had. I was a big girl now, and going to school was so much fun.

After a month had passed, all German schools had to be closed per Polish order. It was a very sad day for me. At the conference in Potsdam, allowances were made for the Polish government to slowly take over managing Schlesien. One of their first orders was to close all German schools.

Adults were talking about what to do about food and clothing, especially in the winter.

The boys always brought home useful stuff. We had a wooden barrel in the basement that Wolfgang had brought home one day. He filled it with sand; he was planning on storing carrots in the sand. He had also found a bin for potatoes.

Not far from where we lived were several potato and wheat fields. All the fields were guarded by Russian soldiers. When the potato harvest came, the boys volunteered to pick potatoes. The boys would make sure to leave some potatoes on the ground. In the evening, when it turned dark, they would go and do their own harvest. Soon, we had a bin full of potatoes.

Getting into the wheat fields was more difficult. The boys watched the guards from afar and noticed how they would meet, smoke a cigarette, and leave the fields unattended. That is when the boys ran deep into the fields, with scissors and a sack in hand. Staying low, they cut and cut the spikes of the wheat stalks. They did this several times. Frau Groher knew how to process the spikes to make flour. First, we let the spikes dry in the sun, then we rubbed them between our hands to make the grain fall out. We used plates and shallow bowls to rub the kernels into. We had to blow, and with the help of the wind, we got rid of most of the wheat chaff before grinding the kernels into flour.

The boys had also found several coffee grinders. Frau Groher adjusted each to a finer grind. We ground the wheat kernels several times. The finished product was whole wheat flour. Mutti had some regular flour that Mara had given her. Frau Groher made a sourdough starter. In a few days, we had fresh baked bread—one large loaf for us and a smaller loaf for Frau Groher. What a treat!

Mutti was very strict about not eating anything that was not cooked or properly washed. I had found a green apple; it was not ripe and it wasn't washed, but I ate it anyway. Mutti could tell I had eaten something because my mouth was all sticky. She asked me several times what it was, but I would not answer. She got so upset and worried that I might get sick. She smacked my mouth several times, but still I would not answer. So she brewed some "Wermut Tee" (wormwood tea), which is a natural remedy for digestive problems. It tastes very bitter. Mutti made me drink all of it. I had never seen Mutti so angry with me.

Our birthdays (Wolfgang's on January 27, mine on August 9, Inge's on October 11, and Mutti's on October 30) were celebrated as best as we could, with little homemade gifts and many hugs and well wishes for the coming year.

One night, we could hear a loud commotion downstairs at the front door. We could hear Russian and German speaking. Then we could hear people running up the stairs, then trying to break into the apartment. We were so scared! Mutti got out of bed and pressed herself against the door to the apartment, hoping to keep the soldiers from breaking in. Wolfgang and I hid under the covers. Inge knew what the Russians wanted. So she opened the window, jumped out, and ran up to the Russian billets to get help. On the way, she met the military police. They came to the apartment and took the three drunken soldiers away. Mutti and Inge felt safe again.

In the apartment below lived the family, who never spoke to anyone in the building. They were the ones we could hear speaking to the soldiers. They most likely told them about our family living upstairs. At the time, I thought the soldiers wanted to rob us. Later, I understood that they probably would have raped Mutti and probably Inge too.

Although we had fresh water and some electricity, sanitation and water purification were almost nonexistent. The word spread quickly that there was an outbreak of typhoid fever, a highly contagious disease. The disease didn't care who you were; it spread through Russian soldiers, Polish, and German people alike. Everyone had to be inoculated. Dr. Larisch, once the doctor for the city's ambulance service, came to the neighborhood to give the shots in three stages. Only Inge had a reaction to the vaccine; she had a headache and a slight fever.

August gave way to September, and the days were growing shorter, a reminder that colder days were not far off. The boys had a plan to steal some coal at the train station. Close by the station was the locomotive shed. Here, the tenders full of coal were kept. The boys befriended some of the young guards, some not much older than Marschall, as Hans liked to be called. They joked and climbed on top of the tenders as part of their plan.

One evening, they waited until it was dark, took the wagon, and went to get coal. Next to the shed was the Mausloch (mouse-hole tunnel). It was narrow and went deep below the tracks to the other side. The boys crawled through the tunnel to get unseen to the shed. After filling the sacks with coal, they planned on going back through the mouse hole. They did not count on the night guards, but they could hear them now driving around the station. The boys barely made it back to the passage without being seen. After a long wait, they made their way back home, leaving the coal behind in the tunnel but going back to get it the next day. Mutti gave Wolfgang a serious talk. He was not allowed to go out after dark again. No more coal-stealing for Wolfgang.

Before Mutti and Vati were married (May 14, 1932), they often went to an operetta, a light opera, or the Kino (movie theater). One of the operettas, "Frederika," had a catchy tune. Vati liked it so well that he would whistle it whenever he picked Mutti up from the taxi company where she worked as a secretary. Eventually, it became the family whistle. We all knew it; even the extended family and our friends knew it.

One day in autumn, we could hear this tune through the open window. An old, shabby-looking man came walking down the street, whistling our tune. Mutti and Inge looked out of the window, then both ran down the stairs out the front door, almost pushing the man to the ground. It was our Vati. He had come to Brieg to find us.

People would write their new address on the house or rubble they used to live in. So did Mutti, in the hopes our relatives would try to find us, and that is how Vati was able to find us. Vati's brother, Willi, Marie, his wife, and family had lived for a long time in Bayreuth, West Germany.

After the excitement had died down, Vati told us his story. He had been in Stuttgart for training when Germany capitulated. He then hid with some farmers and finally made his way to Bayreuth, where he hoped we would be. He had to walk a lot and stopped to do farm work for food and shelter. After he got to Bayreuth, he turned himself in to the US military authority. He spent two weeks in a POW camp. There, he got plenty of food and rest. At his discharge, he also received an ID card. He was able to get a ration card with his new ID. All food, whatever was available, was rationed. He stayed with Willi and Marie.

By chance, Vati met a former co-worker who had not left Brieg as we did. Mutti had talked to him one time after we had returned to Brieg. He decided to move to the west as the Polish government started taking control of Schlesien. He went to Bayreuth; he knew that many people came with the Lazarett Zug (hospital train) that transported wounded soldiers to Bayreuth. That is how Vati found out where we were.

So Vati decided to go to Brieg and get us out. It was an ambitious plan. There was no public transportation going anywhere. He planned on walking all the way, hoping to catch a ride whenever possible. He had to have food to take on the road, sturdy shoes, and a warm coat. He joined the Communist Party. He hoped the membership card would help him through Russian- and Polish-controlled Germany. Again, he walked many miles, mostly at night, to avoid being caught and detained. He would rest in abandoned homes, under bridges, wherever he could find a safe place. He had to make his food last since there was none to buy. Sometimes he would get a cup of soup from a stranger or a potato to supplement the food he had in his pack. He became used to begging. He had to cross streams and fields, always avoiding being caught. He finally made it to Schlesien and then Brieg.

After a few days of rest, Vati devised a plan for us to leave Brieg and go to Bayreuth. Passenger transportation did not exist. His plan was to walk to Bayreuth, the way he had come, to Brieg. Vati wanted us to have as much protection as possible. He applied for a visa from the Polish government to leave Schlesien. To our surprise, the Polish authority granted the request without any further questions.

We also needed a way to haul our few belongings and food. Vati found a carpenter who agreed to make a two-wheel push cart big enough for our few things and for us to ride in when we got tired walking. The man knew Mutti had worked at Moll and figured she had leather. That is what he wanted for payment. Mutti told only Frau Groher of our plan.

The boys had found a sack of dried sugar beet chips. Frau Groher knew how to distill spirit out of the chips. Vati thought it would help to bribe a guard we might encounter. He had us take a taste; it was yucky. We had three bottles of the stuff.

The fourth one Vati gave to Frau Groher for all her help.

The day for our departure from Brieg was set for December 7, 1945. Our pushcart was going to be done the day before. Mutt made sure we had food to take with us on the long journey. Most of our clothes were freshly washed and still hanging in the attic to dry, as were our walking shoes.

Expulsion from Brieg

Two nights before we were supposed to leave, we could hear this terrible noise coming from the street. The front door of the house was kicked in, and heavy footsteps came running up the stairs. Our apartment door was also kicked in, and several Polish soldiers rushed into our apartment. One of them aimed his rifle at the kitchen light and shot at the light bulb, yelling, "Deutsche Schweine raus (German pigs out)!" What confusion in the dark!

We got dressed in a hurry. Vati dumped the straw of one of our mattresses on the floor and set it on fire so we could see. He then stuffed everything he could get his hands on into the sack. It was not much because most of our better things were still up in the attic. Each one of us was responsible for a piece of our belongings to carry. We had practiced when we got ready to go on the seventh. Mine was a small bag with some food. Vati made sure he had the visa, hoping it would help. The whole house was in an uproar. Soldiers are commanding everyone to get out into the street. As we came outside, we could see all the people in the neighborhood being kicked out of their homes. No one was allowed to stay. So we held on to our belongings and got in line with the rest of the people. Teddy was supposed to go with us too, but I was never able to get him from the attic. I missed him for a very long time.

We could hear people asking, "Wo gehen wir hin? (Where are we going?)" The answer was, "Deutsche Schweine gehen bei Gleiswagen nach Deutschland (German pigs are going by rail car to Germany)." Someone said, "Wir sind in Deutschland (We are in

Germany)!" A soldier pushed the man with his gun and shouted, "Das ist jetzt Poland (This is now Poland)!"

It started to get daylight when we finally were told to follow the guards. We were going to the train station. Mutti was carrying a bag with some food and the bottles of alcohol in one hand and holding on to me with the other. Inge and Wolfgang walked in front of us, behind Vati. One of the bottles fell out of Mutti's bag and rolled down the ditch. We could not pick it up; it was too dangerous to be noticed by the guard.

As we came closer to the train station, we could see a long row of freight cars. Soon we found out that was how we were going to travel—shipped out like cattle. The guard started loading the cars with people and their few belongings. When one car was full, the doors were bolted shut from the outside.

Vati tried to get the guard's attention to show him our visa. The guard just shoved him aside. It was our turn to get into one of the cars. We were lucky to be the first to get in; we could get a corner space so we could huddle together. Standing room only. There are no benches, not even some straw on the floor. More and more people were pushed into the car. We saw a woman with a baby in a buggy in one corner. As soon as the car was stuffed full of people, the door was shut and bolted. There was hardly any room to move. After hours of waiting, the train finally moved. People noticed the train was going in an easterly direction and were worried we would be shipped to Siberia. All of a sudden, the train stopped, then changed direction. I could hear a sigh of relief from Vati; we were now going in a westerly direction.

It was dark in the car. The only light that came through the cracks in the walls. So did the cold air. There was no toilet or even a bucket that could be used. It was decided that we would use one corner close to the door as our toilet. But the train stopped often enough so we could relieve ourselves outside. There was no food or water. The train would stop, and the locomotive would be taken to another train. We never knew how long we would have to wait until the train moved again. This happened several times.

The baby in our car cried all the time, probably because it was hungry. People got annoyed with it, but the mother had nothing to feed the baby. The air in the car was being used up, and some people fainted. Sometimes the guards would open the doors and let us go outside.

Vati gave us a sip out of the bottles now and again. Someone saw this and wanted a sip, then another, and another. The bottle was empty in no time. This also happened with the second bottle. Mutti also shared some of our food. She had baked some gingerbread-like bars for our trip to the west. We had to keep this a secret; otherwise, people would have begged and maybe even stolen our provisions. Mutti would give us little pieces and make the bread last for a long time.

We still could hear the baby; it was whimpering now, as if it were going to sleep.

It was very quiet in the car; people were dozing off, and the air was stale. Suddenly, the mother cried out a heartbreaking scream. The baby had died; there was not enough oxygen for its little lungs.

When our bottles were empty, Mutti would collect the water droplets and the condensation of the engine when we were stopped on the tracks. To do this, she had to climb up on the engine and stand there for a long time. She had the bottle almost full when she was ordered back into the car. Everybody begged for a drink.

There was not much left in the bottle for us when she finally made it back to our corner. Once again, the train had stopped. The doors were opened, a sign we learned that we would be standing on the tracks for a while. We could see a few houses in the distance. Mutti grabbed a bottle and started running toward the little town. She was hoping to get some water for us to drink.

As she later told us, she knocked on several doors with no answer. But then a door opened, and an older woman asked her to come in. She gave Mutti a glass of water; she wanted to know what was going on and all about the train. She then filled Mutti's bottle with water and wished her well.

The engine of the train started up again, but no Mutti. The guards made us climb back into the car—still no Mutti. We were so worried that the train would take off and we would never see our Mutti again. Then we saw her running across the field toward the train. We motioned for the guard to keep the door open so Mutti could get in. She made it, breathing hard from running and clutching the bottle filled with water.

The train was moving again. I must have dozed off. Then it came to an abrupt stop that woke me up. The doors were opened wide, and we were told to get out and bring our belongings out too. As we came outside, we could see a very long line of people beside the train, stomping their feet in the snow to keep warm.

The line of people started to move a few steps at a time. Eventually we found out that the train had stopped at the Lausitzer Neisse, a contributory to the Oder River. It was and still is the border between Germany and Poland. Vati realized we were going to the Russian-occupied sector of Germany. All the refugees had to get past the Polish guards. The soldiers checked everyone's baggage. Most people didn't have much to show, but the guards took whatever they wanted. One woman had an old fur coat; they took that and most of hers and her children's clothes too. They stood in the cold, almost naked. No one helped for fear to be treated in the same way. Later, we learned the woman and her children jumped into the ice-cold water of the Neisse River.

One old lady was holding on to her purse. She probably kept some money or photos, her only possessions. One of the guards pushed her into the snow as he grabbed her purse.

Finally, it was our turn to be searched by the guards. Vati showed our visa to one of the soldiers to let him know we had planned to leave on our own. He looked at the paper; it was green in color. He checked to make sure it was an official Polish visa. He waved us through without rummaging through our bag, which Vati was carrying over his shoulder. I guess he could tell there was nothing in the bag that he wanted.

It was so cold, and we were so very hungry but off we went. Vati up front, then Inge and Wolfgang, followed by Mutti and me holding her hand. We followed all the other people, knowing we were close to the Lausitzer Neisse.

Then we saw the bridge we had to cross to get to the Russian sector of Germany. As we came closer to the bridge, we could see it was a railroad bridge made of wooden beams. Again, Vati went first, and we followed. It was dangerous to walk across this bridge, like a trestle. There were spaces between the beams, and we could see chunks of ice floating in the river. To me, it seemed like a never-ending walk.

My short legs could hardly reach across from one beam to the next. One wrong step would have been fatal. Mutti held on to me really tight. It would have been much too dangerous to carry me. We could hear screams that meant someone had fallen into the river, but our family just kept on walking. Slowly, we made it to the other side.

The day had turned into evening, and it was getting dark. We were now in the Russian-controlled sector of Germany. Soldiers led us to a gymnasium. Here, we spent the night. One of the refugee coordinators showed us a space among all the other people who had come here before us. I don't remember getting any food, but we might have.

The next morning, we learned that we had spent the night in the town of Forst. The gymnasium was packed full of people. They had come all night long. Many had frost bites on their hands and toes from having to stay in the cold for hours. Vati's sister, Lotte, was one of the people who came at night. We did not see her again for several years.

We were told to line up. The coordinator explained that we were going to different locations. Our next destination was a refugee camp in the northern part of Germany, in the Russian-occupied sector. Once again, we were transported like cattle on a freight train. We rode for hours, followed by another long walk. It had started to rain, and we were again hungry, tired, and now wet.

We arrived at our destination, the camp. We had been in and out of freight trains without being given any food or water for five days. Now we were supposed to live in a camp. As far as I and my family could remember, the name of the camp was Ventschow (Fenschow). To describe the camp in one word: miserable. There was a long row of metal buildings; some of them had smoke coming out of a pipe on the roof. A soldier pointed at us and walked us to one of the buildings. As we walked in, we saw a large group of people wearing different kinds of clothing. Later, we found out they were ethnic German people from Russia. They were brought to the camp because of their background and the war with Germany. They were considered a threat to Russia.

We were assigned two cots for the whole family. The soldier also pointed to the loft along one side of the barracks, where we could also sleep. Later in the day, another family, a mother and her two children, came, and we had to give up one of the cots.

In the middle of the barrack stood a large oil drum with a stove pipe sticking up through the roof and a square hole cut in front. This was the stove to heat the barracks. We could see fire burning on the makeshift stove. Fire means warmth. We were not allowed to go and warm our hands. We were not welcomed by the people already there.

A soldier came and gave us a meal ticket for five people. We had to go to the camp kitchen to get our meal. We were given a metal bucket and five spoons. That's all we really needed. We get food once a day. It was a watery soup with some chunks of potatoes, carrots, or turnips. That was it—no meat, no bread. We sat on the floor to eat. I had to stand because I was too small to kneel and reach into the bucket to spoon out the soup. Mutti always made sure that I could get my fill. We remembered Mutti's gingerbread bars; they were all gone.

Vati got a hold of a pencil and made a number "1" in front of the "5" on the meal ticket. That meant we would get soup for fifteen people. We got away with this sham for only one meal. Vati was lucky not to be punished for cheating.

Mutti and I slept on the cot. Vati, Inge, and Wolfgang climbed up to sleep in the loft. There was some straw to sleep on, no pillow, no sheets, not even a blanket. We used some of our coats and spare clothes to cover up and keep warm.

The first night at camp was horrible. An old man was lying on his cot in a corner. He moaned and screamed all night long. The next day, we watched him pick off lice and squash them with his teeth. We learned he was blind. He died after a few days.

Guards came around every day, checking for dead people. They carried the old man outside and laid him on the ground. Later, a truck came by and hauled him away with other dead bodies. Then they were dumped into a deep pit. This was a daily ritual.

Several of the other people in the barrack felt sorry for us and let us get warm by the stove. Their lives were not much better than ours.

Mutti, always resourceful, tried to get work in the kitchen, maybe to get some extra food. She was not allowed to work. Vati was a smoker; he would collect dry leaves and roll them into a cigarette, light it on the stove, and smoke, starting to cough with the first puff.

Sanitation did not exist. We had no soap or even water to wash with. Across the barracks was a large field. That is where we had to go because there were no facilities. Most people waited until dark to use "the toilet," so did we. There was no paper, not even grass; it was winter.

We were also infested with lice. Vati and Wolfgang have shorter hair, but not so much. Mutti, Inge, and I had so many lice that we itched and scratched all the time. Someone lent Mutti a pair of scissors, and she cut our strands of hair to get rid of the lice and nits.

I missed Teddy so much. I had to leave him behind in Brieg when we had to get out of the apartment in such a hurry.

When I was a little girl, I used to suck my middle and ring fingers of my right hand before I went to sleep. Now I wanted to do it again for comfort, but my hands were so dirty that I thought better not. I also wanted to be a big girl and not worry about my parents.

Vati walked to the camp office every day, hoping to get information about our stay in the camp. One day, he came back all excited. He had found out that in some larger towns, a refugee transport was being planned to take people to the British-occupied sector of Germany. No one could tell him when and where this was going to happen. So our parents decided to find a way out of camp and get to the West.

Some of the Russian soldiers were bored and happy to try out their knowledge of the German language. Vati befriended one of the soldiers in the office. Seeing our Polish visa, he offered to check us out, but it would have to look legitimate; that meant we had to be checked out by the camp nurse. This all had to be done secretly because we wanted to get away. We were thankful that the soldier offered to help and did not want him to get into trouble. It was close to Christmas, and security was not so tight. Some of the guards were on furlough. This was the signal for us to get ready to leave. The nice lady who lent us the scissors helped us again. She had a little soap so we could clean up and wash our hair. Mutti cut even more of our hair to get rid of the lice and nits. We gathered our few belongings and walked to the camp office. The nurse checked us over. Vati and Wolfgang first—they had the least number of lice. Then Inge and me. Mutti still had so many lice that we hoped the nurse would let her go with the family, and she did.

We all breathed a sigh of relief as we walked through the gate.

It was Christmas Eve, December 24, 1945, and we had no place to go. We were dirty, hungry, and cold again, but we were free. We had spent five days to get to the camp and two weeks in the camp, but where to now?

The plan was to get to the nearest town and find a place to stay for the night. Then we work our way to Wismar. That is where the refugee transport was supposed to leave from.

In town, we saw a Gasthaus (inn). We could see the lights in the window. We stopped to ask for a room. The people were not very friendly, but they let us have a room. Later in the evening, we could hear the owner and his family singing Christmas songs, celebrating the holidays. We knew this family, like all the other people at the time, did not have a lot of food or heating fuel, but they were not refugees as we were.

It made us sad to be away from our home at Christmas. We did not know where any of our relatives were or if they were still living.

The next morning, we walked to the train station, hoping we could catch a train that would bring us closer to Wismar.

Everything was being controlled by the Russian Komandant (commander) for this area. Efforts were being made to normalize life for the German people and for the Russian soldiers.

At the train station, we met an elderly man. He worked for a dairy, collecting milk from the nearby farms. He loaded the heavy milk cans on the train to be shipped to the nearest dairy.

He reached into one of his coat pockets, pulled out a little sack, and handed it to us. To our surprise, the little bag was filled with Pfeffernüsse, little round spice cookies like gingerbread. It was not just food; this was a very special Christmas treat for us. I do not remember the kind man's name. He told us there would be a train going after the holidays. He also asked us to wait, saying that he would be back. After some time, he returned and offered to take us to his house, which he shared with his two sisters.

We could not believe our good luck. The two sisters were so generous. We were able to clean up with soap and warm water. Then we had a lovely Christmas dinner. We were invited to spend the night. Before we went to bed, Mutti washed some of our clothes. We slept in the attic room in two large beds with thick feather covers and pillows. The next morning, the sweet ladies cooked hot cereal for us. I used to never like to eat hot cereal, but this was the best cereal I had eaten in a long time.

These helpful people offered to let us stay. They offered to take care of us children while our parents went to the city to find out about the refugee transport to the West. We spent two more days with these kind people. Wolfgang went with the man and helped him with his work. Inge did some work in the kitchen. Being the youngest, I could just sit in front of the fireplace and enjoy the warmth.

After our parents came back, we spent one more night with our generous friends. I wish I could remember their names.

We packed our few belongings. One of the ladies gave us a rucksack (backpack). Vati did not have to carry the old mattress bag over his shoulder anymore.

They also filled our bag with some food, like bread, boiled eggs, and boiled potatoes. Anything they could spare, and some cookies. I can clearly see the bag. It was made from different shapes and colors of leather.

A sadness came over all of us as we said good-bye to our charitable friends. We all had tears in our eyes, every one of us, but we had to go. The man walked us to the train station, and we hugged again.

It was a long train ride to Wismar. The transport was not ready. We were taken by one of the coordinators to a village close by. It was fun riding in a horse-drawn buggy. He stopped at a lovely house, but the people were not so nice. The man looked us over and said, "Müssen Sie wirklich während den Feiertagen hier her kommen? (Did you really have to come here during the holidays)?"

Vatie answered, "Wenn es zu viel ist uns aufzunehmen waehrend den Feiertagen können wir ja ein paar Tage im Strassengraben verbringen (Well, if it is too inconvenient for you to take us in during the holidays, we will spend the next few days in the ditch across the street).

"Warten Sie (wait here)," was the man's answer as he closed the door.

After a while, we were allowed to come into the house. He led us into an empty room, except for an upright piano. The village coordinator came back later with some mattresses and blankets. His wife had also sent a bowl of potato leek soup. It was so good.

We had to stay there for close to a week. The man talked to us in a friendlier way. I suppose this was his way of apologizing for being so snobbish. The woman was very nice and made sure we had some food to eat. She talked with Mutti and wanted to know all about us. Where we came from and how long we have been on the road. How we got along during these terrible times. She would say, "Nicht meinem Mann sagen (Do not tell my husband)" when she gave us a treat.

One day the man gave us a little Leberwurst (liverwurst sausage), saying, "Nicht meiner Frau sagen (Don't tell my wife)."

Again, we had to leave. This time back to Wismar. It was nighttime when we arrived at the station. We saw many refugees who all wanted to go to the West. Red Cross volunteers told us the train would go in a few days. They escorted us through town to a building. We walked up to the second floor and laid down on the floor to sleep.

Among all the refugees who were staying at this building was a woman who was mentally ill. She wandered around all night. She screamed or sang, then cried or rummaged through people's belongings. We must have fallen asleep. We did not hear her take our food bag. Vati woke up and found her using our food bag as a toilet. She had defecated and ruined the little food we had.

Vati was ready to kill her. It took several people to hold him back, not to hurt the poor, sick woman.

As it got daylight, we could see that part of the front of the building had been blown off by bombs. After this incident, without our food or the unsafe building, we made our way back to the train station. Many refugees were waiting. We sat down, as did all the others, on the stairs going down to the tracks. Cold and hungry again. The Red Cross did its best to feed us, but it was never enough to go around.

After another two days sitting around on the stairs in the train station, we finally got to board the train to the west.

We had no calendar or radio and really didn't know what date of the year it was. It must have been the third or fourth of January, 1946.

This time we were going to travel on a passenger train. One family at the time walked through the gate to board the train. Our family had a compartment to ourselves. Smaller groups had to share. It took a long time until the last person boarded the train. Then we could hear the train whistle, and the train started to move, slowly and then going faster and faster. The steady clickety clack of the train and its warmth made us drift off to sleep. After we woke up, we were able to use the toilet on the train. We rode for a long time.

Then, to our surprise, Russian soldiers came through the train with pushcarts loaded with food. Bread, salami, cheese, and hot tea.

We were so hungry. Mutti gave us this stern look, speaking in her most serious voice: Wir nehmen das Essen nicht an (We are not taking any of this food)." She said, "We had been given very little food since we had to leave home and even less in the Russian camp. Now that we are almost in the West, they feel like feeding us. They can keep their food. We will be taken care of real soon."

Vati slept through most of this. He had a fever and coughed all the time.

The train moved again, all through the night. During the day, we could look out of the window. It was so much fun to walk around on the train. Most of the time, we sat and watched the scenery fly by.

We even got a glimpse of the North Sea-Baltic Sea Canal. Wolfgang knew how a canal was used and explained it to me.

At last, we arrived at our destination: Husum, a town in Schleswig-Holstein, a German state that shares the border with Denmark.

We were greeted by friendly nurses. They checked for sick people. Vati still had a fever, and he was taken immediately to the hospital in Husum. We did not see our Vati for a very long time.

British soldiers escorted us to another camp. But what a difference! First off, we got some hot food and tea. Wolfgang ate three bowls of ham and pea soup, and he got sick.

There were showers for mothers with children and separate ones for men. It felt so good to be under the warm water of the shower. Next, we went to be deloused. The nurse had a metal can with a pump attached, and we got sprayed with powder to get rid of the lice. We did not have clean clothes, but it still felt good to be clean, knowing we would be rid of the lice soon too.

Again, we had to stay with other refugees in camp, a long row of Quonset huts. The huts were clean, had electric light, and were warm. On either side, along the walls, we saw beds arranged on the floor. Mattresses with clean sheets, pillows, and warm blankets. There were families already in the hut. We took the next four beds available in line. We went to sleep clean and with a full stomach, a feeling we had not experienced for some time.

The next morning, a nurse came by and explained to Mutti about Vati's sickness. He was diagnosed with typhoid fever, a highly contagious disease. He would have to stay quarantined in the hospital. She also gave Mutti the address of the hospital and the name of a nurse who she could contact to find out more about Vati.

Wolfgang somehow knew how much I missed Teddy. How he did it, I don't know, but he had found a small wooden ball the size of a large wooden ball. He also had a scrap of fabric and a piece of string. He covered the marble with the fabric and tied it with a string. Then he drew a face on the ball. He gave it to me, smiling and saying, "Das ist für Dich zum spielen. (This is for you to play with.)" I had a little doll! I named her Puppe (doll), and I carried her with me all the time. She was small enough to fit into my coat pocket. It was one of the most precious gifts I have ever received. Mutti was able to wash and mend our clothes.

After a few days, we were transferred to Wester-Ohrstedt, a village not far from Husum.

Herr and Frau Kröger didn't look all too happy when they were told by the Red Cross volunteer that we were the family who would be staying at their house. We were led into a room off the hallway. It was sparingly furnished. There were two beds along the wall, a table in front of the beds, and two chairs. Wolfgang and I would always sit on the bed to eat.

We were told the toilet, an outhouse, was in the backyard, just around the corner of the house. On one side of the room was a small cook stove and a cabinet with some cooking utensils and dishes and some food stuff. Just enough to get by. On one side of the stove was a crate for fuel to cook and keep the room warm. The stove did not put out much heat. We slept two to a bed and put our coats on top of the blankets to stay warm.

The next day, Mutti went to the grocery store to buy what she could get with the ration cards the Red Cross lady had given us. It was a small store with little to buy on the shelves. The grocer lady could sell us some bread and potatoes. She also told Mutti about the dairy at the end of the village. We could get milk there several times during the week.

It was hard to keep the room warm. We only had green wood to burn. Our food had to be on the stove for a long time to get done. We mostly ate soup or potatoes. Good thing we were able to get milk.

At the back of the house was a chopping block. That is where Mutti had to chop our wood for the fire. As she one day chopped the green wood, the little ax slipped and cut into her thumb. I had never seen so much blood; it looked scary to me. Mutti wrapped a sock around it to stop the bleeding. Then Inge went with Mutti to the first-aid station to get help. Wolfgang, wanting to help, went outside to cut the wood. He tried so hard to help, but the same thing happened to him! His cut was not quite as bad, but he too was bleeding.

So Inge walked with him to get his thumb treated. He had a bump on his thumb where the cut had healed until the day he died.

Mutti was able to take the bus to Husum to see Vati in the hospital. Typhoid is very contagious, so he was kept in a room under quarantine on the fourth floor. Mutti could see him only through the window. He was always sleeping. Later, when he was feeling better, we could see him as he looked out of the fourth floor window. He waved at us and went back to bed. Later, when Vati was well again, he told us the doctor treated him with all sorts of shots of medications to make him well and vitamins because he was very malnourished.

Some days, Mutti was able to buy fresh fish or mussels for us to eat when she went to see Vati in the hospital. That was always a feast for us.

It was now one year ago that we had to leave our home in Brieg.

Like all the other birthdays during the past year, we celebrated Wolfgang's ninth, the second one away from our home in Brieg, very quietly. We gave him big hugs, wished him well, and made sure he would get the biggest portion of whatever we had to eat that day.

The Kröger's had a big black dog, a German shepherd. I was very scared of him. I was always afraid to go to the outhouse because, many times, he was outside. As I came around the corner one day, I did not see him, but suddenly, he jumped out of a corner. I ran back into the house. Mutti came with me to the outhouse because I was too scared to go by myself.

Not much happened, but one day a column of British military trucks drove through the village where we lived. One truck stopped, and a soldier got busy working on the truck. I put on my blue knitted hat, the Christmas present from Oma, and walked out to see what was going on. The soldier spoke to me, but I didn't understand English at the time. He smiled friendly, then he reached into his truck and gave me something. Then he drove off again. I ran back into the house, not knowing what the soldier had given me. Mutti remembered some English from school and recognized "milk" and "chocolate." As I opened it, I could smell the wonderful aroma of chocolate. We all looked at it for a long time. Then I had Mutti cut it into four equal pieces so we could enjoy this tasty surprise. She cut my piece a little bigger since the chocolate was given to me. My very first Hershey bar.

Behind the house where we now lived were fields and woods. When the weather was good enough, Wolfgang and I would go scouting. We would find twigs, pine cones, or pretty rocks. We would pretend they were all the things we used to have but now miss. As we were scouting one day, we discovered a hole in the ground, like a cellar, at the edge of the woods. We climbed in and found some turnips. We grabbed a few and put them in the bottom of our pants. We limped home, pretending to be hurt. Mutti was angry; she scolded us for taking something that was not ours. Since it was food of which we never had enough, she kept the turnips and used them in our next meal.

We did not have any toys or games to play with except my little doll. Wolfgang would teach me to count and remember the alphabet. He also made me spell words. During rainy days, we would look out of the window, hoping for the sun to shine real soon.

Inge was so much older that she probably realized how bad the situation really was. She hardly spoke and sulked a lot. We had very few pieces of clothing. Mutti had to wash everything by hand and dry it in our room.

Bayreuth, Bayern, Germany

The plan was that after Vati was well enough to travel, we would try to get to Bayreuth, where Vati's brother, Willi, his wife, Marie, and their family lived.

We remembered Willi and Marie; they stayed with us once for a few days. Willi was in a tank company and hurt his hand. He had a few days off, so Marie came to be with him. Somehow, probably through the Red Cross, Willi found out where we now live. He was able to obtain travel papers for Tante Marie to come and take us children to Bayreuth.

Mutti was not happy with this situation, but Vati was getting better, and so she agreed to let us go, knowing that she and Vati would come to Bayreuth very soon too. There was Tante Marie, loud and boisterous, with a Bayreuther (Bavarian) accent we could hardly understand. Mutti came with us to the train station, and we said a tearful goodbye.

We had to change trains several times and cross the border between the British and American-occupied sectors of Germany. I don't remember much else about the trip because I was so worried about having to leave Mutti and Vati behind.

Finally, we were in Bayreuth. We had to walk quite a way to Jean Paul Street, where they lived. It was a very small house, with two apartments. Willi and Marie had an adult daughter, Anni; she had a daughter named Helga. The apartment was small, with a kitchen and one room on the ground floor and two more rooms on the upper floor. We got one of the rooms on the upper floor. It had two iron-framed beds, a table, some chairs, a stove, a large Schrank, and an old trunk.

The trunk was given to us, and it stayed with our family. Many years later, in 1971, Mutti gave me the trunk as a reminder of all the bad times we experienced. I still have the trunk; it sits, filled with blankets and odds and ends, in the corner of our bedroom.

Helga had several dolls. Uncle Willi gave me one of them. She was dressed all in pink clothes. She had long hair and could close her eyes. She was too pretty to play with. Most of the time, I kept her sitting on the bed. Later, when we moved to another place, Helga took the doll away from me. After a while, Uncle Willi brought the doll back, but it did not make me as happy as when I got the doll the first time.

There was no bathroom like we had at home. It was more like a latrine or outhouse, only inside the house on the upper floor. A shaft connected the seat with the pit in the ground. I was always scared to go because of the big, dark pit way below. Wolfgang called it the "Plumps Klo" (plumps toilet) because when you had to go number two, you could hear it go "plump."

We had to help Tante Marie in the kitchen, make our own beds, hang laundry, and do other everyday chores. We still had time to play outside and get to know the other children in the neighborhood. Inge met a boy she liked; Wolfgang made friends with boys his age. There were no other girls my age except Helga; she was two years younger than me. She was not fun to play with. She didn't share her toys and had a fit if someone touched her things.

So I tagged along with the boys. We played tag, hide, go seek, and "Drive the Farmer off His Land." To play this game, you had to have a little kitchen knife and a patch of hard dirt; the bigger, the better. We would mark off an area as big as possible and draw a line through the space to make two or more even sections, depending on how many kids would play. The first player would hold the knife by its tip and toss it to hit the ground. If the knife stuck in the ground, the player then marked off the piece of land as his after he erased the connecting line. Sometimes the knife didn't stick in the dirt; there was no new land for the farmer. Wolfgang was good at this game.

He tried to teach me, but I never quite lost the fear of throwing the knife.

We patiently waited for Mutti and Vati to come to Bayreuth.

One day we were outside playing, and we could hear the tune we all knew so well. There they were, Mutti and Vati, walking around the corner. I kicked off my shoes and ran as fast as I could, not minding the rock and bits of glass on the plaza I had to run across to get to my parents.

Vati was still very weak from being so sick and not getting enough protein, fruits, and vegetables in his diet. His legs were swollen. He had a hard time walking because his feet barely fit into his shoes.

It did not take long for us to work out sleeping arrangements. Mutti and Vati got one bed, and Inge and I got the other. Wolfgang had to sleep on a cot that had to be stored under the bed during the day.

Mutti learned from Tante Marie where to apply for food ration stamps, for clothes and shoes, for just about everything. She also got a voucher for pots, dishes, and cooking and eating utensils. The plates and bowls were red enamel with a black rim. We also got glasses— beautiful red glasses. One of the neighbors gave Mutti a milk pitcher. It was white with blue cornflowers. It was one of the few nice items Mutti had. She used it for many years, even though the cornflowers had faded. After her death, Wolfgang kept and used it.

At first, Mutti would cook our meager meals in Tante Marie's kitchen, but she decided to just cook in our room. Mutti did not like conflict.

Someone had told Mutti of Caritas, a Catholic outreach organization that helped the poor and needy. The Lutheran Church in Bayreuth worked with Caritas to help refugees and people who had lost their homes during the bombing. This was the place to get help. Caritas received and distributed care packages. Generous Americans donated food, clothing, and money to help people in need. Frau Giegler, the deacon's wife, oversaw distributing goods in our area, and she made sure we would get our share of whatever was available.

We were lucky to get all sorts of good things, like spam, corn meal, dried milk, and egg powder. We were not familiar with some of the items, like egg powder. Mutti quickly learned how to use them. There was also a treat for us: sweet and vanilla-flavored ice cream powder. We did not know what it was at the time, but it was a treat. Mutti would ration it out by putting two tablespoons of powder in a red glass, one for Inge and one for Wolfgang and me. We would dip our fingers into the powder and enjoy the sweet treat, seeing who could make the treat last the longest.

Bayreuth was heavily bombed during the last days of the war—four allied attacks—two heavy and one light US attack as well as one very heavy British attack. These bombing attacks destroyed more than 36 percent of the living spaces, homes, and apartments, along with 32 percent of industry and historic and cultural buildings.

To find an apartment where we could move too was next to impossible. Besides, refugees were not welcome; some people called us foreigners. Others accused us of bringing disease or stealing their belongings. In some cases, refugees were treated like criminals. Citizens with large houses or apartments had to sublet some parts of their homes to people who were bombed out or to refugees.

One day, after we had lived at Jean Paul Strasse for several weeks, Frau Giegler told our parents of two rooms that were available to sublet. Two elderly sisters lived in this five-room apartment. The Housing Authority assigned one room and the kitchen to the sisters, Frau Feiler (a widow) and her sister, Faulein (Ms.) Veiland.

One of the rooms was already in use by a couple and their son. We got the other two rooms and kitchen privileges since we were a family with children. But the ladies were so afraid we would harm them that they locked the kitchen door very early in the evening. So after we got a stove, Mutti decided to cook in our room and only get water in the kitchen. One of our rooms used to be the dining room and was furnished accordingly, but all the doors and drawers of the china cabinet and sideboard were locked. Mutti had them take out the side board and make Frau Feiler empty part of the cabinet for us to use.

Our new address is now Kanzlei Strasse 4 (Chancellery Street). Across the street, there were government buildings.

In time, we got some furniture. Bunk beds, a dresser, a wardrobe, and some chairs.

Our parents slept on two old chaise lounge sofas, one on each side of the room, below the windows in the main room. The best thing about this room was the big table and six chairs. The whole house had electricity, except for this apartment. The owner didn't care to have it. We had a gas lamp above the table, but not in the children's room.

There were also flush toilets in the building, but again, the owner did not want one.

The bathroom was half a flight of stairs down from where the apartment was. There were two small rooms, but no bathtub. We had to carry water to flush and use an oil lamp when it got dark. Still, it was a giant step up from having to go in the open field or the Plumps Klo.

The gas came on at 5:00 a.m. and stayed on for several hours. Then it was shut off until the evening. It came on again in the evening for several hours so people could cook and have light. We did not cook with gas but used the lamp above the table. After the gas was shut off again in the evening, we used a kerosene lamp. The knob of the lamp had to be turned off so the gas could not escape when it came back the next morning.

One evening, we were probably telling stories or reading, and we did not remember to turn off the lamp. The next morning, when the gas came back, our parents almost died of carbon monoxide poisoning. Vati was able to open the windows and place Mutti so that she could get plenty of fresh air. They both recovered, but we always made sure the gas was turned off.

Vati got a job from a man, whom he knew from Brieg, as a detective. It was mainly finding relatives and friends or displaced people. No criminal work. He worked with the Red Cross and the police. This is how he found Oma, Tante Emmy, and her children. After many letters to the authorities, Oma was allowed to move permanently from the Ost Zone (the Russian-occupied German sector) to West Germany. It was so nice having Oma live with us.

We got another bed, and I got to sleep with Oma. She explained how they got out of Brieg, hoping to get to Dargun, Mecklenburg, to stay with Tante Emmy's sister-in-law. They were caught in the middle of fighting as the Russian army advanced into Berlin. They were trapped for several days in the root cellar of a farm. They could hear the tanks rolling above as the fighting kept up. Everyone, mostly children, women, and old men, was scared. They waited another night, once the fighting had stopped, before going outside to see what was going on. The farmhouse was in rubble, and the barn was in flames. It took several hours to dig out of the cellar. They searched for food but found little. Somehow, they made it to Dargun, only to run into more trouble with Russian soldiers fresh from the front lines fighting. Some were decent; others raped and plundered. Edith had delivered a baby just days before; they found her in bed and raped her. They grabbed Emmy, but Oma offered herself, but the soldier pushed her aside and took Emmy. Russian soldiers ripped wedding bands from women's fingers. Oma's ring finger was stiff where a soldier had ripped off her rings. Hers and our Opa's ring, which she always wore together, was a sign of being a widow.

Summer came to an end; it was time for school to start. I could hardly wait for September 3, 1946. On my last birthday in August, I turned seven and was a year older than most of my classmates, all girls. Classes for boys and girls were in separate wings of the school. In the beginning, we only went three days a week to school in three different schools, including Saturdays. Two of the schools were close to where we lived. It took thirty minutes of walking to get to the third one.

School supplies were hard to find. I was lucky someone had given me a slate and a writing stick. The slate had a crack, but I could still use it.

Wolfgang had to have a notepad. We had to collect bits and pieces of paper because, to get a notepad, you had to have two pounds of old paper to trade for a pad. There were not enough school books, so we had to share them with our classmates.

I remember my first-grade teacher, Fraulein Fenske; she was very tall and a refugee. She was very helpful and understanding. She would write our lessons on the blackboard for us to copy. We also had to learn things by heart, like the alphabet, counting, and doing easy math problems in our heads. Frl. Fenske would have us play number games to make learning more fun. I was able to get a notepad and didn't need to do my homework on the cracked slate anymore.

We also had to learn to speak and write in complete sentences. We always had some homework, making up for only going three days per week to school. One assignment was to write ten complete sentences.

Oma had told us the story about her brother Ernst not doing his assignment of writing a composition but reading it from his notepad without a word written down. This really impressed me, and I thought I could do the same with the sentences. When my turn came to read to the class, I did fine, starting out with sentences one, two, and three until I got to the tenth sentence. There, I had to stop reading, not remembering a word.

The teacher had a look at the empty paper and just shook her head. I could tell she was not angry. As she turned to the black board, I could see a smile on her face. She had me write the sentences and show them to her the next day. She also wanted to know who gave me the idea, so I told her the story, and she made me tell my parents what I had or hadn't done.

One of the best things about school was that all the children were given hot, cooked food once a day. Mostly soups or stew-like meals, but always plenty. Many times, we were able to bring food home because some children didn't like it or had enough food at home. On Saturdays, we would get hot cocoa and Brötchen, crusty rolls I liked so much. The kitchen lady always gave the leftovers to the neediest children. Wolfgang and I were among them.

The food was sent to Germany by the Quaker Society. It was called "Quaker Speise (Quaker meals). Every time I see the picture of a Quaker on some food package, I am thankful these good people sent food to us when we needed it the most.

After living in the apartment for a while, we noticed bite marks on our arms and legs, practically all over our bodies. Oma recognized them at once: bedbugs. It seemed that they liked me the best. Mutti wrapped my arms so I would not scratch all the time; besides, she didn't want other children to make fun of me.

Vati talked to Frau Weiland; she accused us of bringing them to her home. Then he went to the health department, and our rooms were fumigated. Everything was fine for a few weeks. But then it started all over again—more bedbugs and more bites. Vati notified the health department again. After a thorough inspection, the inspector ordered the whole house to be fumigated. Even the wallpaper was pulled off the walls to do a thorough job. This was done during the summer months so the house could be aired out after the fumigation, but still, it smelled bad for a long time.

We had made friends with the children in the neighborhood. One of our friends lived across the street in one of the government buildings. His father was the manager of the government buildings. Behind the buildings was a big courtyard. There were coal sheds, bike racks, and a Teppichstange (carpet rod), two tall poles connected by a cross bar. Cleaners used to hang their rugs on the cross bar to beat the dust out of them and clean them.

All the children would gather and play in the courtyard. Wolfgang had climbed up onto the crossbar, and a boy chased him with a long pole. Wolfgang lost his grip and fell to the ground. He tried to get up but could not; he had broken his right arm. I ran like the wind, yelling, "Mutti, Mutti, Wolfgang hat seinen Arm gebrochen (Mutti, Mutti, Wolfgang broke his arm)!" I could not get up the stairs fast enough. Mutti helped Wolfgang up the stairs, made a sling, and walked with him to the hospital.

A long time later, she came home alone. The doctor determined that Wolfgang had broken his elbow and kept him in the hospital for observation. After several weeks, the cast was removed, and Wolfgang had to go to therapy.

Figure 5: Wolfgang and me, 1948

He said it was painful, so he asked the doctor if he could go swimming as therapy. The doctor thought this to be a good idea, and Wolfgang swam every day in the fire department water supply pool. By the end of the summer, he could straighten and move his arm like before.

Food and fuel, like wood and coal, were still rationed. Mutti had an old bicycle; she would ride to the farm villages and ask for potatoes or other foods. She offered to pay. Sometimes she could buy; other times, the farmwomen would give her one or two potatoes. Other times, she was chased off the property by the farmer and his dogs.

Mutti and Oma would go to the woods to collect pine cones and dry sticks for kindling to cook our food. It was harder to find anything, as many other people had done this too. One day, as they were collecting kindling a black man, an American soldier stepped out of the bushes, which startled Oma and Mutti. He smiled, took Mutti's little ax, and cut down a small tree. He cut it into manageable pieces, loaded them on the cart, and covered them up with dry branches. Mutti and Oma talked about this many, many times.

I wanted to help, too. One day in the summer, I went blueberry picking in the woods. No one knew where I was. My little bucket was half full as I started to go back home. I was hungry and had eaten almost all the berries by the time I got home. Everyone was happy that I was safe home again. Vati had me sit down and gave me a talking to, never to go off by myself. I was also not allowed to go out and play for a whole week.

Many people from Brieg lived in Bayreuth. They had come with the Red Cross train that brought wounded soldiers to safety at the end of the war.

There was a friend Vati found one day who was a tailor. When we got some coupons for fabric, he made a suit for Vati and, from some of the remnants, a skirt for Mutti.

Frau Giegler would also bring clothes that were sent in per-care packages for needy people. There were some nice, usable items. I remember getting several dresses and some sandals; I had to save them for school. There were also cocktail dresses and fancy shoes with high heels—not what Mutti needed at all! She cut off the heels of the fancy shoes; that did not work at all. When she tried to walk, she would be rocking because of the way the shoes were constructed. It was sad, but we all had a good laugh anyway. Somehow, she got another pair of shoes. I used the funny shoes for play. Most of the clothes we got were usable, and we were thankful to get them. We thought it was generous for people to send clothing to Germany.

On April 3, 1948
The Marshall Plan was initiated
To provide aid to war-torn Western European Countries

Oma knew how to knit all kinds of things—mittens, hats, scarves, gloves, sweaters, and even stockings. People had heard about her talent and asked her to knit for their families. She did and asked for yarn as payment; this way, she had yarn to knit things we needed.

She taught Wolfgang and me how to knit. Wolfgang was good at it. He knew how to knit five-finger gloves.

We didn't see much of Inge. She had a boyfriend and was gone a lot of the time. She had a real hard time dealing with how our lives had changed because of the war and the aftermath.

School resumed in September. I was happy to go back and be with my classmates. One girl, Erika Schneider, was my best friend. It was hard to visit with her during the summer since she did not live in our neighborhood. We were very close and always sat together during class. She was very talented and could draw beautiful pictures. She was a persnickety eater and would always give me some of her food. I would repay her by helping her with spelling and arithmetic problems. Her parents were nice people. Many times, they would give me some fruit or vegetables to take home. Erika and I have been friends for life. She lives in Hungary now with her husband, Georg, and we keep in touch by phone.

All summer long, we had to go barefoot. I cannot remember how many times I stubbed my toes or stepped on a little piece of glass on the street. I promised myself that if we could buy shoes again at will, I would never ever go barefooted again, only if I wanted to. This promise still holds.

> On June 20, 1948 the Waerungsreform
> (Devaluation of the Reichsmark)
> Reichsmark was replaced with the Deutsche Mark
> In the US, UK, and FR occupied sector of West Germany
> At the rate of 10:1 (1:1 for cash and accounts)
> Reichsmark was changed to the Ost Mark
> on July 28, 1948 in the USSR occupied East Germany

We were eligible for financial aid since we had lost all our belongings and money because of the two times we had to leave our home and everything we owned behind.

At first, we had only paper money and no coins. I remember the 10 Pfennig being blue in color with a white edge. I found one laying on the street one day. I saved it for a long time. Then one day, an ice cream cart was outside on the street, and I proudly walked up and bought myself an ice cream cone.

Many people, especially men, were out of work. So was Vati. The office where he worked as a detective closed. Most people found their relatives through the Red Cross.

Men and women worked on clearing up rubble from the massive bombing that had destroyed so much of Bayreuth. Vati was not strong enough to do this kind of labor. He kept on looking for our relatives. He found his two sisters, Gretel and Lotte. To our surprise, Lotte was married again to an US Army soldier, an officer, Sedrick Laughlin.

Lotte knew where Gretel and Opa Seidel were living in the East Sector. After writing many letters, they got permission to move to West Germany. Opa, with his second wife, came to Bayreuth to live. Gretel and her son Peter stayed in Bad Hersfeld, where Lotte and Sedrick took care of them until Sedrick was transferred back to the US.

Lotte and Gretel had also been sick with typhoid fever, like Vati. Lotte and Sedrick were generous and helped with food and clothing as much as they were able to.

Once again, summer came to an end, and we went back to school. We had classes every day now at the same school. Wolfgang and I went to Graser Schule (school). There was a small park across the street from the school with a bust of Johann Babtist Graser (1766–1841), a well-known educator. Later, when I was a teenager, I used to meet my boyfriend, Günther, in the little park. There were benches to sit on, and we could watch the Red Main, one branch of the Main River, flow by.

St. Nikolaus Tag (Santa Claus Day) is celebrated on December 6. I was not so sure there was a Santa Claus, but then there was a knock on the door. When I opened the door, there he was! I recognized the coat he was wearing and his voice. I was supposed to say a prayer, recite a poem, or tell Santa if I was bad during the year. I stood there and did not say a word. He threatened to take me away in his sack, and still I did not say a word. Mutti and Vati urged me to speak, but to me, this was not Santa Claus, and so I just stood there.

Santa gave Wolfgang some treats because he had answered some of the questions. Santa then picked me up and put me in his sack. He slung the sack over his shoulder and walked out of the apartment down the stairs. Mutti came running after us, begging Santa to let me go because I really was a good girl most of the time. So Santa let me get out of the sack but warned me to be good and behave. He did not give me any treats, but Wolfgang shared his with me.

When next year's Santa Claus Day came, we had a most unusual surprise. I knew now that there was no real Santa Claus. When the doorbell rang, I answered, and to my surprise, there was St. Nikolaus—a tall man dressed in a fancy robe; he wore a bishop's hat and carried a tall staff. He also had a helper, Pelzemaertel. He carried the sack with gifts. Even Wolfgang had a questionable look on his face. St. Nikolaus wanted to know about school and asked many questions. We answered them all. Then he had his helper give us some treats, say good night, and leave. To this day, no one in our family has ever found out who this St. Nikolaus really was.

Christmas was always a happy time for us. We were happy to get handmade presents. Oma would knit mittens or a sweater with whatever wool she could get. I made tree decorations by cutting stars, snowmen, and other shapes out of paper, then coloring them to decorate our little tree. Wolfgang made an Advent calendar; it had five windows, one for each Sunday and Christmas. There were fun little pictures in the windows, like a snowman, a lit candle, Santa Claus, and a comet star. In the Christmas window, he drew the Nativity scene. I do not know how she did this, but Mutti managed to save enough ration stamps so we could have a lovely meal for Christmas. She baked some stollen, a sweet Christmas bread, and some cookies. We also got nuts, apples, and oranges.

Oma had two brothers, Fritz and Ernst, who had immigrated to the US. Her brother Fritz left home at an early age—before WWI started. He worked as a ship steward for several years and then decided to make New York his new home. In 1922, he married Maria, a woman from Hungary.

After the war, Ernst, his wife Rosa, and their son Willi moved to the US. They also lived in New York. Rosa had two daughters from her first marriage. They joined them after Ernst and Rosa were established, had good work, and had a home.

Oma was in contact with her brothers for many years up until WWII, when Hitler prohibited all contact with the US. Oma, Ernst, and Rosa tried to find each other through the Red Cross after the war. One day the long-awaited answer came with Ernst and Rosa Konietzky's new address, and Oma was so happy to have found them. Ernst was diagnosed with arthritis, and the doctor suggested he move to Florida. They chose Miami; that is where they lived for the rest of their lives.

One day, Oma received a drop-down picture postcard about Florida from Rosa. I used to study this postcard. There were pictures of palm trees, flamingos, hibiscus, and orange trees, as well as the beach. I would look at the pictures, thinking this is paradise; one day I will live there; as you know, I did for more than twenty years.

I still have the postcard and look at it now and again.

Not all was good news. During the many years without contact, Fritz had died, as had Maria, his wife.

Oma lived in West Germany long enough to be able to have her own place to live, a one-room apartment. The housing department sent her to Frau Lienberger, an elderly widow who had a five-room apartment. Two rooms were already rented to a couple. Oma got one room with kitchen and bath privileges. Frau Lienberger was happy to have another widow living in the apartment. She gave Oma some chairs, a wardrobe, and a table. I liked the chairs so much, so Mutti gave them to me after our Oma passed away. I still have one of them. Frau Lienberger also gave Oma a copper Bundt cake pan, which I still use. Oma preferred to have a little stove for heat and to cook her meals in her room. She would visit us almost every day, but I still missed her. I would spend many weekends with her. She always cooked boiled potatoes with butter for me, one of my favorites. She taught me how to play gin rummy. Some nights, we played until midnight. But she still made me get up Sunday morning and go to church with her.

Life had become more normal. Very slowly, ration cards were phased out. Clothing stores had more inventory. Newspapers were printed again. We did not need scrap paper to get school supplies. There were enough school books available for every student.

I really liked school. We went to school Monday through Saturday from 08:00 to 12:00. On Monday, Wednesday, and Friday, we had additional classes in the afternoon from 14:00–16:00.

We had a fifteen-minute break during morning classes. If the weather was suitable, we would go out to play on the girls' side of the playground. On rainy days, we stayed indoors and played games. Morning classes were mostly academic. Several times a week, we had language, social studies, arithmetic, geography, history, biology, penmanship, and religion classes.

Afternoon classes were taken up by sports like swimming, gymnastics, track, and field. We also had needlework one afternoon every week, where we learned to sew, embroider, crochet, and knit. Later, English was offered as an elective subject.

On alternate Mondays of the week, we had music. We learned about composers, especially about Richard Wagner, the renown opera composer. He lived and worked in Bayreuth. The class made a field trip to the Festspielhaus (festival hall), which is what Wagner named the opera house that he designed himself.

Only Wagner's operas are allowed to be performed there. We also learned about Franz Liszt, a composer and piano virtuoso. He also lived in Bayreuth. Both Wagner and Liszt are buried in Bayreuth.

On the other Monday, we had art. There too, we learned about painters and their works. We also had to do drawings and work with water colors. My work was never better than average. Erika, my best friend, had a talent for drawing and painting. She made beautiful pictures. We were also tested in both music and art; this is where I made up for not being artistic. I liked to read about the artist and was able to answer most of the test questions.

We also had sports classes. During the winter months, we had classes in the gym. We also learned to swim in the city's indoor pool. During the summer months, we had classes outdoors—track and field and ball games.

My favorite subject was history, but I also liked math and geography. My weakest subject was penmanship. We also learned to write the old German way; the letters were like artwork. Once a year, each class would go on an Ausflug (field trip). We would visit famous castles or churches, have a picnic, or eat at an outdoor restaurant.

Twice a year, we get report cards. Our participation in class, written work, and homework were given grades on a scale of 1–5. One being very good, 2 being good, 3 being satisfactory, 4 being shortcoming, and 5 being insufficient, you failed the subject. My grades were always very good, except for penmanship, where I usually got a satisfactory grade during the first few years of school.

Later, as my writing improved, I was happy to earn a good 2 in handwriting. The teacher always wrote a comment about the student's behavior and how well he or she progressed.

Report cards had to be signed by a parent and returned to school. Vati always signed mine. I know he was happy about my grades, but like parents do, he always thought that there was room for improvement.

On Sundays, we would attend Kindergottesdienst (children's service) church services for children, like Sunday school, at the Lutheran Church, the Stadtkirche (main city church).

Once again, Frau Giegler came to talk to our parents. Her plan was to help the family. She knew of a lady who was moving to live with her daughter. This lady, Frau Hoffman, used to have a small business of washing, starching, and ironing men's shirt collars. Those were still worn by many elderly men. Frau Giegler thought that was something our parents could do to supplement Vati's unemployment income.

We would also have to move to the house where the shop was located. Our parents decided that would be a move to better our lives. It was Mutti who would do the work with Vati's help until he found another job. Vati had always worked in government offices. It was hard for him to get a position since he too had lost all his papers. He needed witnesses to prove that he was never an active member of Hitler's party, the NSDAP.

My parents agreed to Frau Giegler's proposition. We moved to Kolpings Platz 3. Now we had two rooms, a small kitchen, and a little storage room below the staircase. The toilet was again an outhouse behind the main house. That's also where the water faucet was located. The house belonged to the city. Not long after we moved there, Vati requested that a water faucet and sink be installed in the hallway of the house so the other families in the building could use them too.

We had no more bedbugs.

We live close to Grasser School now. There were other children in the neighborhood. Sometimes, during summer vacation, we would play outside. One of my favorite games to play was Kibble Kabble. We used a piece of wood about six inches long and carved the ends to be tapered to a point so the ends would not touch the ground. With a long stick, we hit either one of the ends of the Kibble. Once it was in the air, you had to hit the flying Kibble to make it fly farther. Some of the kids could hit the stick four or more times in a row. Once a player lost the kibble, the next player could play. I could never do more than two hits.

German people like to celebrate Fasching (the carnival season) every year. Starting the day after Epiphany and ending on Fat Tuesday at midnight before Asch Mittwoch (Ash Wednesday) at the beginning of the Lenten season. It's a fun time. Many events are held. With parades, formal balls, children's parties, costume balls, and Kappenabend (cap evening), where everyone wears a funny cap, the family of my friend Erika had a large enough room to hold a children's party. We had a good time playing games, dancing, and having special Kichla doughnuts filled with jam. There is a picture of me wearing an imaginary costume.

Figure 6: Kinderfasching: children's carnival, 1951

When I was older, my boyfriend took me to the Rose Ball, one of the formal events during the Fasching season.

Someone gave Wolfgang a very old men's bike with a crossbar from the seat to the handle bar. He worked at it, cleaned and oiled it, and got it to run. He painted it bright orange, then he used a candle and made burn marks all over the frame. It looked great.

I learned to ride on this bike. It was hard for me to get my short legs over the bar to reach the pedal on the other side. Once I was on the bike, it was just as hard to stop and get off again. To make it a little easier, Wolfgang turned the seat around when I used it. That gave me a little more room. I fell several times and had scrapes and scratches all over my legs. I still have a little scar where I fell and landed with my right leg on the cog wheel; it bled and bled for a long time.

Eventually I was able to ride, but I always needed a step up to get my leg over the bar, and the same for getting off again.

Somehow word got around, and Mutti started to get many more customers. It was hard work getting the water from the outside faucet to the washhouse in the back building. German households, at the time, did not have washing machines. Many of Mutti's customers wanted all their laundry to get done.

Vati still didn't have a job. The decision was made to find a better and larger location for the business. The building was in a more affluent area of town. With the help of a loan, a large industrial washing machine, a laundry spinner, a Mangel (ironing roller), irons and ironing boards, a heater for the drying room, and other necessities were bought for the shop. For several years, the business went well. Vati stopped looking for work, and they hired a woman to help with the work.

Our Oma would cook for us and help in the business. Wolfgang and I were expected to help as much as possible. Wolfgang, on his bike, would deliver finished laundry to some of the customers. He liked this job; some customers would give him a tip. I worked, with Oma's help, on the mangel. The machine could iron flat pieces like sheets, tablecloths, and such.

In time, German people could buy all kinds of kitchen machines, including washing machines. The business fell off, and it was closed. It had been the bread and butter for our family for several years.

Vati was finally able to get a good-paying position with good health insurance and a pension plan with Farmers Insurance, a government agency.

I have not mentioned much about Inge during the years I wrote about how our lives went. She had distanced herself from the family. Vati would talk her into coming home many times. She always left again after a short while. Once she was of age, she stayed away for several years. In the end, she came back home, and all was forgiven. She died of stomach cancer in 1992.

There is a school photo of me. It was taken in 1950, several months before I had my eleventh birthday. It shows me with pigtails and a braided little crown on top of my head. I also wore my little gold heart-shaped earrings I got for Christmas and one of my favorite dresses. It was made from multi-colored plaid fabric with a white collar. Best of all, it had two pockets, one on either side of the dress. The picture shows me smiling. It was a very happy time for me and the family.

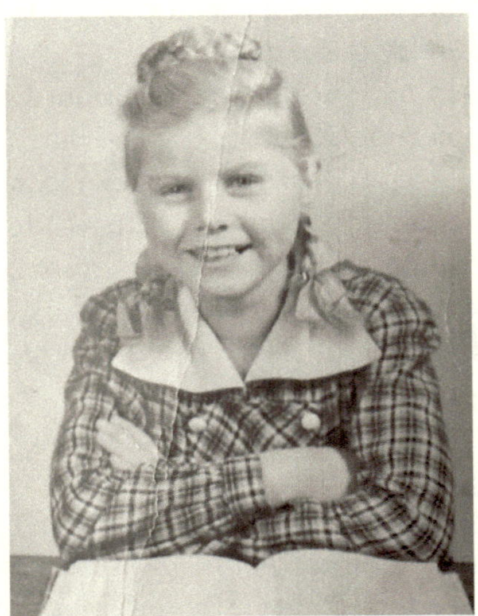

Figure 7: School photo, 1950

With this, I will end my story. I told you how happy and how difficult or sad the first ten years of my life were. Mutti was our rock and my heroine. Because of her strength, our family has survived these uncertain years. The influence of my parents, Oma, and my teachers helped shape me into the person that I am today.

With love, Mutti, Momma, and Mom.

Acknowledgements

I would like to thank my daughters for so patiently waiting for me to finish writing my story.

I would also like to thank my husband, who encouraged me to keep on writing.

About the Author

Edeltraud Seidel Evans was born in 1939 in Brieg, Schlesien, Germany, which is now Brzeg, Selesia, and Poland. She came to the United States in 1963 and became a US citizen in 1968. After living in various states, she now lives with her husband in Indiana.